MASSACHUSETTS
BOOK
OF THE
DEAD

GRAVEYARD LEGENDS
AND LORE

Roxie J. Zwicker

THE
History
PRESS

Published by The History Press
Charleston, SC
www.historypress.net

Copyright © 2012 by Roxie J. Zwicker
All rights reserved

First published 2012

Manufactured in the United States

ISBN 978.1.60949.757.6

Library of Congress CIP data applied for.

Contents

Introduction

Dear Ancestor

Your tombstone stands among the rest
Neglected and alone
The name and date are chiseled out
On polished stone.

It reaches out to all who care
It is too late to mourn,
You did not know that I exist
You died and I was born.

Yet each of us are cells of you
In flesh and blood and gone
Our blood contracts and beats a pulse
Entirely not our own.

Dear Ancestor, the place you filled
One hundred years ago
Spreads out among the ones you left
Who would have loved you so.

INTRODUCTION

I wonder if you lived and loved,
I wonder if you knew
That someday I would find this spot
And come to visit you.

—Anonymous

Thank you for joining me as we take a journey through the fascinating past of the cemeteries of Massachusetts. By picking up this book, it's clear that you must be a bit curious about burial grounds. Maybe it's the allure of the hand-carved gravestones, or perhaps it's the stories of the cemetery ghosts. Or maybe it's just the opportunity to connect with and honor our history. Whatever has attracted you, get ready to journey through the variety of cemeteries the Bay State has to offer.

I grew up in the Pioneer Valley of western Massachusetts, and I had always wondered growing up who the pioneers were. For me, that term always referred to settlers traveling westward to places like Texas or Oregon. I quickly learned after a series of local school field trips and self-conducted explorations (which I did when I was older) who the pioneers in my neighborhood were. I found them in the old cemeteries, and I read their stories on their gravestones.

There was so much of Massachusetts that I wanted to see when I learned how to drive. When I got my first car, I visited the large cities and small towns from the Berkshires to Cape Cod. The temptation to explore these towns' cemeteries was pretty strong. Granted, fall in New England is really beautiful, and you can take some of your best photographs in the cemeteries where there is often a wide variety of colorful trees. But once the pictures were snapped, it was almost irresistible to shuffle through the fallen leaves and look at the gravestones closer.

Some of the cemeteries I visited were so old and forgotten that, sometimes, I thought people may not have visited there for years. Others were meticulously kept: the pathways were clear, and the stones were in good condition. On some trips, I'd stop at the local bookstore and see what I could find for cemetery history books. I often felt that when I found a cemetery book, I was pretty lucky, as there were not many of them out there. Before I knew it, I was cataloging cemetery photographs and researching some of the more interesting stones. The more work I did, the more I found and the more enticing it became.

I have amassed literally tens of thousands of photographs of gravestones and cemeteries, and often when I'm planning a trip, I'll search out the locations of the cemeteries before I even make hotel reservations. When I return home, I carefully look through the photographs and information that I've gathered

Old rusty gates and fences show off their salty air patina in Vineyard Haven.

from the trip. My car has many scuffs and scratches from driving down remote dirt roads just to find an elusive gravestone.

When I'm putting together cemetery presentations or writing about them, I often picture the people from the cemeteries I've visited standing behind me while I'm at my computer doing my work. Sometimes, I imagine them each saying, "Tell my story" and "Don't forget me." My goal has always been to keep their memory alive by telling their stories, and while I know I can't tell everyone's story, I strive to tell tales of both the famous and the not-so-famous.

In this book, I will unearth the tales of many people whose lives have been summarized in a few sentences on stone. Join me as I wander the rows of gravestones and markers and discover the legacies and ghosts of these Massachusetts cemeteries.

Chapter One
Discovering Historic Massachusetts Graveyards

From my rotting body, flowers shall grow and I am in them and that is eternity
—Edvard Munch

It all began with 102 Pilgrims, all of whom were Separatists from the Church of England who had fled to the New World where they could worship God as their consciences dictated. After a long and dangerous passage across the Atlantic Ocean, they landed at Plymouth, Massachusetts, on December 21, 1620.

The Pilgrims were hardy, industrious and God-fearing and were prepared to face every kind of danger and suffer every affliction without complaint. They struggled through their first winter in the New World while maintaining their faith in the wisdom and goodness of God. Within just a few weeks of arriving in Plymouth, half of the Pilgrims had died; everyone had become so ill over the harsh winter that there were only a handful of people well enough to keep the settlement going. The colonists dealt with death nearly every day, and burials occurred almost as often as religious services were held.

The earliest grave markers in Massachusetts were stones and boulders, and it was thought at the time that these would keep the dead from rising out of their graves. Some also believed that if plain, unmarked stones were used, the Native Americans would have a difficult time finding the graves.

In some cases, many of the first markers were made from wood planks or rough stones, but these usually did not last very long after being exposed to the elements. As more burials occurred, it became necessary to indicate on the markers who was buried there, and it then became common practice to inscribe the deceased's initials or name. Over the course of twenty-five years, the colonists established a handful of burial grounds, the oldest of which are in Boston, Plymouth, Salem and Ipswich, Massachusetts.

The grave markers that were used in the mid- to late 1600s were more ornate, reflecting early Puritan beliefs, and the decision was made to start using gravestones styled like the ones in England. In the Puritan view, death was inevitable; it was God's punishment to humankind for Adam's original sin. They believed that evil spirits and evil men occupied the earth, suffering from "utter and unalterable depravity." Children were shown corpses and were taught to fear death. They were also taught that their own parents would testify against them at the Last Judgment. But there was the possibility of salvation; if a Puritan lived and worked during his lifetime to "bring God's kingdom home," then he would be granted eternal life. The Puritans also believed that while people in their society would be able to receive eternal salvation, most faced eternal damnation. It was preached that Hell was a place of "unspeakable terrors."

Those who settled in Massachusetts during the seventeenth century lived in a very simple and yet symbolic world. Using the imagery that surrounded death and funerals at the time, gravestone carvers translated these beliefs, using the ministers' sermons for inspiration. William Cooper, a Boston minister, described the lessons that burial grounds were supposed to teach the living: "Look into the grave and see a dead body, that has been buried there but a month or two, all covered with darkness and corruption, and say whether it is suitable for one to have high thoughts of himself." Most burial grounds were set up just outside churches and meetinghouses, so people could get a firsthand view of their own mortality just outside the windows during lectures and sermons.

Early gravestones became one of New England's first folk art forms. A variety of skulls, crossbones, winged hourglasses, pickaxes and shovels were just a few of the most common symbols carved on the earliest gravestones in Puritan times. These symbols, unaccompanied by text, served as reminders of death. The belief was that people who passed by the burial grounds and saw these very stark reminders of death would be moved to ponder their own existences on earth. Puritans who regarded death as God's punishment for sins would often tremble with fear on their deathbeds, afraid that they might suffer eternal damnation in Hell. Some stonecutters, however, added more than just symbols of death and carved dramatic scenes of death imps carrying coffins away. Gravestone images depicted life's stories in stone, communicating moral lessons or spiritual truths. These gravestones were (and, to some extent, still are) more than just memorials of the dead; they were messages to the living.

In Orleans, an original gravestone from 1725 stands with its more recent granite copy.

There are several primitive-style gravestones in the Boxford Village Cemetery.

As new cities and towns were established during the eighteenth century, the number of burial grounds increased. Many parcels of land next to churches and meetinghouses were set aside for burial purposes. There were many who elected to be buried in small family plots on the land where they lived, but unfortunately, many of those graveyards have been lost to time and urban development.

At some point during the eighteenth century, beliefs about death and cemeteries began to change. Death was no longer seen as a terrifying consequence of sin; rather, it was viewed as an opportunity to be reunited with your loved ones who had already passed. This shift in attitude, consequently, ushered in changes to gravestone design, as angels and cherubs replaced grinning skulls and images of the grim reaper.

During the American Revolution, the British buried their fallen soldiers in the spots where they had died. Historians still have not been able to pinpoint where in Massachusetts these graves lie.

The cemeteries grew almost as fast as the towns, and by the late 1700s, some graveyards had become so overcrowded that bones and coffin fragments would wash out of the graves during rainstorms. There was an immediate need at the turn of the century to establish new burial grounds, and changes were in store for the cemeteries of old. By the early 1800s, cemeteries were landscaped to look more like the picturesque gardens of England, turning them into places of peace and serenity rather than fear.

The first garden-style cemetery in America was established in Cambridge, and it was called Mount Auburn. Many other cemeteries were built in the style of this cemetery, and many of the old colonial burying grounds were forgotten as people looked to the new cemeteries to build grand monuments of remembrance.

Today, there are a variety of burial grounds throughout Massachusetts, and each offers a unique landscape and history. And each gravestone has a story to tell about those who passed before us.

Chapter Two

An Early Landscape of Death

Colonial Burying Grounds

OLD NORTH BURYING GROUND (HIGHLAND CEMETERY), IPSWICH

The town of Ipswich was originally named Agawam after the natives who lived there. In the native tongue, the word means "a place where fish of passage resorted." In *The History of Ipswich, Essex and Hamilton*, it reads that in 1614, Captain John Smith described Agawam: "Here are many rising hills and on their tops and descents are many corne fields and delightfull grouse [grounds]. On the east is an isle of two or three leagues in length the one halfe plaine marish ground fit for pasture or salt ponds with many faire high groues of mulberry trees. There are also okes [oaks], pines, walnuts and other wood to make this place an excellent habitation."

The town was settled in March 1633 by John Winthrop Jr. and twelve others, and a year later, it was named Ipswich. In 1638, Masconomet, the Indian chief of Agawam, sold the land to Ipswich for twenty pounds. He died twenty years later, at which point, most of his tribe had become extinct.

The first people interred in the burial ground were the wife and child of John Winthrop Jr. There are a few colonial court judges, including Colonel Samuel Appleton, who died on October 30, 1725. His gravestone displays a fascinating coat of arms. He once presided over a complaint against Sarah Cloyce for "sundry acts of witchcraft." Sarah was later imprisoned in Salem. He also once heard a confession by Arthur Abbott, who stated he had exaggerated claims of witchcraft against Elizabeth Proctor. Elizabeth's husband, John, was one of the victims of the Salem witchcraft trials and was hanged in 1692. She was released from prison in May 1693 when the hysteria finally came to its end.

The burial ground offers everything from simple fieldstone markers to elaborate hillside tombs with climbing stairs. One of the most moving gravestones found there belongs to Sarah McKean. She has a portrait-style stone that features a carving of a woman with a shroud around her. Just below the woman's arm is a small carving of a baby that is lying on its side, its hand across its chest. The inscription reads:

Erected in memory of
Mrs Sarah McKean wife of
Mr William McKean Daur of Doctr Jos Manning
who departed this Life May 15ᵗʰ 1776
Ætatis 33
How loved how valued, once avails the not,
To whom Related or by whom begot,
A heap of dust alone Remains of thee,
'Tis all thou art and all the Proud shall be.
surve ye this well ye fair ones and belive,
The grave may terrify but can't deceive
Yet vertue still against decay can win?
And even lend mortality a Charm.
Also Sarah McKean Dau'.r of Mr Willm & Mrs Sarah
McKean born June 24ᵗʰ 1771 Departed this life Octor
6ᵗʰ 1775

Stylized flowers, leaves and spirals can be found on the grave of Reverend Belcher, who was a preacher at the Isles of Shoals in New Hampshire. He later moved to Newbury, Massachusetts.

Here Lies Ye Body
Of Ye Reverend
Samuel Belcher
A Preacher at Ye Shols
Many Years He Was
Cald to Newbury
Newtown & Ther
Lived 18 Years & He
Died March Ye 18
1714 AE. 74

An Early Landscape of Death

A solemn-faced angel can be found on the gravestone of Zerviah Frisbie, who was the wife of Reverend Levi Frisbie:

Memento Mori
Erected to the Memory
of Mrs Zerviah Frisbie
The amiable & virtuous
Consort of the Revd Levi
Frisbie; who departed this
Life on the 21ˢᵗ Day of Augt
A.D. 1778 Aged 31 years & 5 Mon.

Prudent & meek she pass'd the various woes,
Belov'd by friends, uncensur'd by her foes;
Yet worth like this, could not avail to save
One favour'd mortal from an early Grave:
Chear'd with fresh hopes Lifes future bliss to gain
She drop'd—and told us all this world is vain.
Peruse ye happy pairs this speaking stone
And think her fate ere long may be your own.

It is interesting to note some of the strange and accepted funeral customs Ipswich townsfolk practiced during the seventeenth and eighteenth centuries. For example, in 1685, at the funeral of Reverend Thomas Cobbett, the minister in Ipswich, one barrel of wine and two barrels of cider were consumed, and "as it was cold," there was "some spice and ginger for the cider." The climate of alcohol consumption portrayed by the beloved minister's parishioners is hard to imagine, but excessive drinking was quite a common practice in the days before temperance and prohibition. In the case of a pauper's death, the town would provide and bear the expense of intoxicating drinks. A careful and, above all, experienced committee was appointed to supervise the mixing of the funeral grog or punch and to attend to the liberal and frequent dispensing of it to the mourners. There are many tales of spectral visions that were seen by those who just happened to overindulge in drinking during the course of events. Some people in the funeral attendance would often describe seeing the spirit of the deceased walking among the living; whether it was truly a ghost or a drunken delusion can be debated.

The first meetinghouse was built on the hill in Ipswich around 1634, not far from the cemetery, and it is where evangelist George Whitfield is said to have confronted the devil and thrown him out of the church's belfry. The famous devil's "footprint" can be seen imprinted in the rocks in front of the current church, the sixth structure built on the site. In addition, Ipswich has one of the largest collections of original seventeenth-century homes in America. To find the former inhabitants of those homes, take a walk through the Old North Burying Ground to see where they peacefully rest.

CENTRAL BURYING GROUND (BOSTON COMMON BURYING GROUND)

In 1754, the decision was finalized to establish what was known at the time as South Burial Ground. The two-acre lot located in the southeast corner of Boston Common was the fourth burial ground established in the city. The name was changed to Central Burying Ground when a new cemetery was established in 1810 on Washington Street that was to be called South Burying Ground.

This gravestone at Central Burying Ground in Boston warns readers of the hazards of working on a ship's crew. Chow Manderien, who was just nineteen years old, suffered a fall from the masthead aboard the ship *Mac* in 1798.

An Early Landscape of Death

HERE WERE REINTERRED THE REMAINS OF PERSONS FOUND UNDER THE BOYLSTON STREET MALL DURING THE DIGGING OF THE SUBWAY 1895

It is said that over nine hundred bodies were discovered while workers were constructing the subway in 1895.

The first tomb in the Central Burying Ground was built by Benjamin Bas in August 1771. By the early nineteenth century, there were over 130 tombs bordering the grounds. Each tomb was numbered, and many were marked with names. Although there are no records of interments before 1756, gravestones bearing earlier dates have been dug up. In all probability, these stones were relocated to the new graveyard from one of the earlier burial places. A stone was found years ago bearing the following inscription: "To Captain William and Mary, His Wife, Died Aug 24 1794, Aged 14 Days." The upper part is missing, but the lower part of the stone is still on the ground. Another slate gravestone was dug up in July 1906 and bore the following inscription: "Thomas, Son Patience, 3 Months Aug 1 Ye 1729."

In 1895, when the tunnels and the Boylston Mall were constructed, the remains of nearly 1,100 people had to be disinterred to make way for the massive construction project. There were many who were opposed to the construction. The plans, however, were carried out. A letter from the doctor who oversaw the removal of the remains describes the incident in detail:

Boston July 27, 1895
To the Boston Transit Commission
Gentlemen:
The excavations in the Boylston street mall are now so far advanced that there is little or no likelihood that more human remains will be found in that section of the work. Before the digging began it was known that the path of the trench lay along and through a line of tombs which were covered up nearly sixty years ago when the mall was laid out in 1836[,] since which time they have been disused for further interments. For this reason it was anticipated

that many human bones would be found while the work was progressing and on that account your Board on April 18th placed the removal of such remains under my charge. With this preliminary statement I now have the honor to submit the following report.

On April 19th my attention was first called to the discovery of various parts of several skeletons which were found during the forenoon of that day or the afternoon of the preceding day lying outside of the tombs. Steps were taken at once for the proper care of these fragments and boxes were ordered for their final disposition. Apparently the bodies had been placed originally in the ground though there was left hardly any trace of coffins and it seemed probable that many of the bones had been previously disturbed. This incident was but the beginning of the discovery of other remains which continued daily in considerable numbers for several weeks. The various parts of the skeletons were so incomplete that it is impossible now to say with any exactness how many different persons they represented but an approximation to the number is given later in this report. In some cases the fragments were very small and if found elsewhere would not have been recognized as belonging to the human frame. The special duty of collecting these remains was assigned by the contractors to two or three men who I am satisfied did their work faithfully and whenever practicable they placed the bones of one body in a single box. In two instances the Lowell and Tuttle tombs where the remains in tombs were identified… were taken by representatives of the two families and reinterred elsewhere.

During the progress of the excavations it was found that the line of buried tombs extended from a point near the entrance to the Common at the south west corner to a point nearly opposite to the old Public Library. Some of the tombs had been almost entirely destroyed while others were in a fair or good condition. Nearly all contained coffins[,] which for the most part[,] were so decayed that they could not be bandied and the enclosed bones were much decomposed. In many instances the brick arches that once served as the top of the tombs had been broken in and the tombs themselves partially filled with earth bones[,] stones and other matter and then covered over with granite slabs. So confused were the contents that it was impossible to find out the number of original interments. It was evident that such tombs had been used for the reception of bones that had been disturbed in the surrounding ground when the mall was built.

Lewis Jones & Son undertakers have had charge of the reburials which were made in the adjoining burying ground on the Common and their part of the work was done in a satisfactory manner. Fortunately it was possible to find a place in that ground where all the remains could be reinterred in a row by themselves without disturbing other graves.

The following is an estimate of the number of bodies either whole or represented by parts found and reburied.

Taken from seven tombs which had not been previously disturbed—90.

Other remains for the most part previously disturbed and lying in confusion about 820–910.

In conclusion, I wish to acknowledge the help I have received from Messrs Jones & Meehan[,] the contractors Mr. Guy C Emerson[,] an assistant engineer[,] and Mr. Robert M Meehan who have cooperated with me in this matter and have been ever ready to adopt my suggestions.

Through them the work has been carried out in a manner respectful to the memory of the dead and satisfactory to the feelings of the living.

Very respectfully yours,

Samuel A. Green

A simple gravestone lists a summation of the mass grave, but there is not a listing of the names of those interred.

Some reports indicate that the cemetery also contains an unmarked mass grave for British soldiers who died in the Battle of Bunker Hill. One of the most recognized graves in the burial ground belongs to famous artist Gilbert Stuart. Sometimes called the "Father of American Portraiture," Stuart painted the portrait of George Washington that is on the dollar bill. The marble gravestone for Stuart was placed on his grave approximately one hundred years after his death.

According to local tour guides, there is a restless spirit of a sad little girl who haunts the cemetery. The legend says that she has been appearing for many years and can sometimes be seen reaching out her hands toward passersby. Many people have described seeing a child's apparition sitting on the fence, hiding behind the trees or moving about the gravestones.

OLD BURIAL HILL, MARBLEHEAD

Located eighteen miles north of Boston, Massachusetts, is the quaint old town of Marblehead. This scenic peninsula at the southeastern corner of Essex County boasts one of the most beautiful harbors on the North Shore. Officially founded in 1629, the narrow, picturesque streets are crowded with an amazing assortment of historic seventeenth- and eighteenth-century buildings. The land was originally inhabited by the Naumkeag Indians, and the remains of Native American villages, burial grounds, shell mounds and even an Indian fort have been discovered over the years. Additional evidence

Father time is carved on a gravestone from the early 1700s as a reminder of mortality.

This is one of many stones at Old Burial Hill in Marblehead that bear lengthy epitaphs.

such as spears, arrowheads, clubs and a variety of utensils has been found scattered throughout Marblehead.

Fascinating legends and tales creep from the town's history books, and many relate to those who are buried in the old cemetery. There are stories of pirates and buried treasure and also one about a screaming ghost on the beach at Lovis Cove. A ghost ship is even said to sail back and forth across Marblehead Harbor. Out of all the ghostly and curious places in town, none is as legendary as Old Burial Hill, a cemetery that has been the final resting place for the town's residents for nearly 375 years.

Old Burial Hill was founded in 1638 at the site of Marblehead's first meetinghouse. Overlooking Marblehead Harbor, this high point in town is the final resting place of hundreds of Marblehead's first citizens and is also the burial site of an estimated six hundred Revolutionary War soldiers. Only a few of the soldiers' graves are actually marked. Accessible from an entrance on Orne Street and another from Pond Street, the burial ground looms large and sprawls across the top of the granite-faced hill. The ancient slate tombstones lean in every direction throughout the grounds. Gnarled trees with knotholes that seem more like watchful eyes stand guard throughout the cemetery. The tall, twisted trees were merely saplings about one hundred years ago, according to the earliest photographs taken of the cemetery. In their own way, the windswept, crooked trees, as well as the gravestones, seem to help mark the passage of time here.

One of the most curious local legends is that of "Old Dimond," the wizard of Marblehead. Edward Dimond leased a large parcel of land for the sum of thirteen shillings yearly, beginning in 1709. Old Dimond was said to have been able to conjure the power of the sea at will and use it for whatever he needed. Sea captains and townspeople sought his mystical advice, for many believed in his great powers. Whether he got his power from the black arts or his commanding voice alone, he was said to have the ability to bring distress upon his enemies and to help his friends avert disasters. Some people thought that his uncanny ability to foretell the future could shape their fortunes at sea.

On nights when waves crashed on Marblehead's shores, the sky rumbled above and the gale force winds blew, Old Dimond would fearlessly make his way to Old Burial Hill, and the townspeople would hide safely in their homes away from the storm. In between the tombstones of the cemetery, it was said that the wizard would "beat about" them while his voice echoed out over the waters. According to the tales about Old Dimond, no one would dare question his ability to save someone from a shipwreck with his words. Dressed in an indigo cloak and whirling about the tombstones in the middle of stormy nights, the wizard would spend hours in the cemetery controlling the forces of nature. It has even been said that he would shriek to the sailing vessels, "Belay there and harken to the voice of 'Old Dimond!'"

The book *The History and Traditions of Marblehead* (1880) describes the wizard and his relationship with the townsfolk:

> *In April, 1709, the commoners leased all that great head of land on the northeast side of Charles Island in Little Harbor to Edward Dimond, "shoreman," for the sum of thirteen shillings yearly. This person was probably the famous "old Dimond" of whom such fabulous stories were told and believed. It was said that he was a wizard, and possessed the "black art" which enabled him to foretell coming events, to avert disaster from his friends, and bring distress upon his enemies. When the night was dark and stormy, and the wind gave evidence of a blowing gale, "old Dimond" would wend his way to the "burying hill" an there among the graves and tombstones beat about and give orders for the management of vessels at sea. In a voice loud and clear, distinctly heard above the roar of the tempest, these orders would be given, and no one dared question their power to save from shipwreck. The advice of "old Dimond" was sought by people far and near, who believed in his great powers, but woe betide the evil-doer who came into his presence. Once when a guilty fellow who had stolen wood from a poor widow came to him for advice, the wizard "charmed" him, and caused him to walk all night with a heavy log of wood on his back. At another time, when a sum of money had been stolen from an aged couple, "old Dimond" told where it could be found, and gave the name of the thief. Let not the reader think that these stories illustrating the superstition of our ancestors are exaggerated in the least. They are told by aged people, living in Marblehead today, who remember with faith and earnestness they were told by their mothers and grandmothers.*
>
> *Of the same class are the stories told of the man who was chased one night by a corpse in a coffin, and shortly after sickened and died; of the poor fellow who was chased by his Satanic majesty himself, seated in a carriage and drawn by four white horses; and of the young fisherman who arrived home in the night, and meeting the young woman to whom he was betrothed, gave her a few of the fish he had caught, only to see her fade away and vanish from his sight. The next morning the heart-broken lover learned that the girl he loved had died during his absence, and became convinced that he had seen an apparition. What the ghost did with the fish has never been satisfactorily explained.*

Old Dimond's granddaughter, Moll Pitcher, carried on his magical legacy in neighboring Lynn, Massachusetts. She was a fortuneteller and tea-leaf reader, and she attracted many curious visitors from across the Atlantic. Much like her father, sea captains and sailors sought her advice for a peek of their fortunes at sea. She is buried in Western Burial Ground in nearby Lynn.

Nearly two hundred years later, tales of Old Dimond are still being told in and around Marblehead. It is said that on dark nights, the wizard's voice can still be heard yelling commands into the winds that cross Old Burial Hill. Others say that his indigo cloak can be seen moving between the stones at sunset.

In the cemetery, you can find the memorial stone for Wilmot Redd that was placed there in 1998 by the Town of Marblehead. Her small house was next to Old Burial Hill, on the southeast corner of the pond that now bears her name. In 1692, in neighboring Salem Village, Wilmot Redd was among those accused in the witchcraft hysteria. She was described as a crusty old woman with a very sharp tongue who was most unpopular with the townspeople, especially the womenfolk. She was married to fisherman Samuel Redd, and the local fishermen knew her as "Mammy." Wilmot Redd was tried for witchcraft on September 17, 1692. She denied the charges against her but was not allowed

defense counsel. There was no one to speak on her behalf, including her husband. She was condemned to hang on Gallows Hill four days later. It is said that no one came to claim her body, and she ended up buried in an unmarked pauper's grave. Wilmot was the only Marblehead citizen executed for witchcraft.

Along the minsters' row section of the burial ground is one of the most unique headstones in New England. Susanna Jayne's headstone was carved by Henry Christian Geyer, a prolific stone carver from Boston's South End, and it was commissioned by her husband, Peter Jayne. The crown, or top of the stone, has an unusual shape that is well protected in a granite encasement.

This one-of-a-kind gravestone, commissioned by Susanna Jayne's husband, Peter, features bats, bones, a snake and the grim reaper and other symbols.

Among the symbols featured on the stone are an hourglass and bones, which remind us that our time on earth is fleeting. There are also two smiling, winged cherubs to represent the heavens and two bats to represent hell. Encircling much of the carvings is a snake swallowing its own tail, creating a never-ending circle that is known as the uroboros, which symbolizes eternity. The scythe also represented death; the symbolism of the scythe was used to compare men to tall stalks of wheat growing in the fields, and the scythe, like death, would cut them down in the prime of life. The skeleton holds the sun and the moon, depicting the cycle of life and, in some interpretations, the Old Testament and the New Testament. The skeleton wears a wreath of laurels and is wrapped in a cloak or cloth, which symbolizes victory over death and the soul's triumph over the trial of an earthbound existence. The epitaph reads:

> *Deposited*
> *Beneath this Stone the Mortal Part*
> *of Mrs. Susanna Jayne, the amiable Wife of*
> *Mr. Peter Jayne, who lived Beloved*
> *and Died Universally Lamented, on*
> *August 8th 1776 in the 45th*
> *Year of her Age.*

> *Precious in the Sight of the Lord is the Death of his Saints.*

> *Here Sleeps the precious Dust—She Shines above,*
> *Whose Form was harmony, whose soul was Love.*
> *What were her Virtues? all that Heaven could Spare*
> *What were her Graces? all Divinity Fair.*
> *Mingling with Angels, they admire a Guest,*
> *As spotless Good, and lovely as the Rest.*

A monument was erected near the gazebo on Old Burial Hill to commemorate a tragic event. A fleet of ships from Marblehead was caught in a hurricane while those on board were fishing the Grand Banks of Newfoundland on September 19, 1846. Sixty-five men perished, and at least eleven vessels were lost. The fishing industry in Marblehead never recovered from this horrific occurrence.

In 1848, the "Fishermen's Monument" was dedicated by the Marblehead Charitable Seamen Society. It lists the names of the deceased who were lost at sea:

An Early Landscape of Death

LOST
On the Grand Banks of Newfoundland
In the Memorable Gale of September 1846
65 Men and Boys
43 Heads of Families
155 Fatherless Children
"The Sea Shall Give Up the Dead That
Were In It."

Among the many unique details on the gravestones in the cemetery are two stones that display coats of arms. The gravestone for Richard Hawley, who died in 1698, has a coat of arms with fleur-de-lis and scallop shells on it. John Legg's gravestone (dated 1718) has a heart carved on it, and within the design is a diamond that contains a coat of arms with a knight's helmet and a stag.

Down the hill, on the far side of the cemetery, is Joseph Brown's gravestone, which features an eagle and a banner that reads "Victory in Peace." Joseph Brown was known by the locals as "Black Joe." He was the son of an Indian father and a black mother. He served in the American Revolution and eventually became the owner of a very popular tavern in town, which can still be visited today.

There are many gravestones from the seventeenth century in the burial ground, and the oldest one is dated 1681. At the far edge of the cemetery, down the back of the hill by Redd's pond, is the Crocker Tomb, an aboveground crypt and a collection of nineteenth-century gravestones. The secluded area has a seventeenth-century path that runs through the gravestones that is known as Red Ant Trail.

Should you find the scene of the graveyard slightly familiar, you may recognize it from the movie *Hocus Pocus*. This fictional, family-friendly Disney movie, which was filmed in the area in 1993, is about the three Sanderson sisters, who were seventeenth-century witches who were conjured up by unsuspecting pranksters in present-day Salem. The daytime graveyard scene was filmed at Old Burial Hill.

The cemetery is one of the most dramatically situated burial grounds in Essex County and has a great view of the town and the harbor. The gravestones are mostly in very good condition, considering their age. A visit to Old Burial Hill, no matter the season, is always fascinating. Just be sure to bring your camera.

ANCIENT BURYING GROUND (BRADFORD BURIAL GROUND), BRADFORD

Incorporated in 1675, the town of Bradford was originally part of Rowley and was known as Rowley on the Merrimack. The east parish of Bradford (established in 1726) separated in 1850 and was incorporated as the town of Groveland on March 8, 1850. On January 1, 1897, Bradford was annexed to Haverhill.

The parcel of land that was to become the location of the town's burial ground and meetinghouse was given by John Hazeltine in 1665. Located on Salem Street, the cemetery is just about the size of an acre. There are over 850 burials on the ground, and many of the early settlers and four of the first five ministers of the town rest here.

Among the many notable graves in the cemetery is the grave for Nathaniel Thurston, who died in 1811. He is buried beside six of his seven wives. Robert Mullicken Sr., who had emigrated from Glasgow, Scotland, at the age of eighteen in 1684, is also buried in the cemetery. Robert was known for carving geometric patterns of stars, flowers and masked faces on his gravestones. He

The oldest stones in Bradford Burial Ground are located in the trees at the bottom of the hill.

changed his carving style slightly every two years, and his stones can be found in Bradford, Newburyport and other area cemeteries.

The nineteenth-century stones can be found at the front of the cemetery, but if one ventures down the hill, the oldest gravestones can be discovered. Many of the stones are tipped and slanted, but most of the carvings are still legible. Some of the stones even have crude carvings of coffins. Many efforts have been made by the local residents to clean up the undergrowth in the cemetery, and work is still ongoing. In fact, many unknown graves and stones were recently discovered through **GPR** (ground-penetrating radar) scanning.

A few of the inscriptions on the stones are included here:

> *Miss PATTY Crombie*
> *daughter of Lieut James &*
> *Mrs. Mary Crombie*
> *died April 27th 1807*
> *Aet. 18*

> *The youth in bloom with morning smile,*
> *Did late the parents heart begile*
> *Faded in death now pale she lies*
> *And fills the parents heart with sighs.*

There are many mystical swirls on the gravestone for John Everet:

> *HERE LYES BURIED*
> *the BODY OF*
> *Mr John Everet*
> *OF DEDHAM*
> *WHO DIED*
> *June the 20th*
> *1726 AGED*
> *25 Years*

A cherry epitaph is on the gravestone for Jeremiah Gage:

> *Mr.*
> *JEREMIAH GAGE*
> *died,*
> *Dec. 25, 1821*
> *Aet. 68.*

While weeping o'er my silent grave,
My friends, believe it true;
That when you've toiled a few more days,
Here waits a bed for you.

OLD HILL BURYING GROUND, NEWBURYPORT

The town of Newburyport began as a fishing and trading community. Located along the Merrimack River, the scenic town is famed for its beautiful eighteenth- and nineteenth-century architecture. But the town also has its secrets, such as the fact that it was a center for privateering in the eighteenth century. Underneath the city streets are remnants of the old smugglers' tunnels that formed a labyrinth beneath the old homes.

Standing on a high point in town is Old Hill Burying Ground, which was established in 1729 on what was known as Snelling's Hill. Dr. William Snelling was based in town around 1650, and his name is mentioned in a court complaint from 1652 in nearby Salem, Massachusetts. He allegedly made some utterances when he was drunk that offended some of the townsfolk. According to record, he said:

I'll pledge my friends,
And for my foes
A plague for their heels
And a poxe for their toes.

Dr. Snelling admitted his misdeed in court and apologized. He was fined ten shillings and court costs for the incident. Coincidentally, while the documentation is detailed about the court proceedings, there is nothing in the record of deeds that mentions the transfer or sale of Dr. Snelling's property to be used as the burial ground.

Interred in the burial ground are the locally famous, the forgotten and members of the militia. One of the most interesting characters is Lord Timothy Dexter. There has been much written about this man who was referred to as "eccentric" in almost every biography about him. One of his more famous sayings at Thanksgiving time was, "An ungrateful man is like a hog under a tree eating acorns, but never looking up to see where they come from!" Lord Dexter headed up several different business ventures, selling items such as Bibles, coal, molasses and some say even cats. He

Above: The grave for Dolly Picket in Newburyport. The unusual gravestone shows a carved portrait.

Right: This grave in Old Hill Burying Ground in Newburyport features a shovel and pickaxe—the tools of the grave digger—as well as a grim reaper and a dove.

wasn't ever at a loss for money as he had married a wealthy widow of Newburyport.

His mansion was often a place of spectacle, and he even built his own family mausoleum behind it. He commissioned intricately detailed, silk-lined mahogany caskets, and every so often, he would take a daily nap in one of the coffins in the mausoleum. Lord Dexter even went so far as to find out who would show up for his funeral by running his obituary in the paper while he was still alive and announcing the date and time of his wake. It was said that nearly three thousand people showed up to the affair. However, his wife was not interested, and despite his insistence, she wouldn't show a shred of grief. When he finally did pass away at the age of sixty in 1860, he was buried in Old Hill Burying Ground under a simple marble gravestone with an urn on it.

In an 1896 book called *Ould Newbury*, there are several mentions of the burying ground, along with a handful of gravestone photographs. The gravestone for Deacon Parker Noyes is mentioned in great detail, as it is such an unusual stone. It is described in the following manner:

> *Among the noticeable gravestones in this old burying ground is one erected to the memory of Deacon Parker Noyes. It is of light gray color, tinged with yellow, and bears an inscription cut with unusual care and skill. The elaborate scroll work, with the figures representing angels, at the top of the stone, the shape and style of memorial letters, and the ornamental border of oak leaves and acorns surrounding the inscription…The alphabetical lists beneath the inscription, were evidently placed there to show the ability of the stone cutter, and perhaps, incidentally to advertise his work.*

The photograph that accompanied the above paragraph showed a variety of finely detailed lettering at the bottom of the stone, with both uppercase and lowercase letters displayed in alphabetical order. The stone was dated 1787 and also included the inscription, "The immortal part quick left its frail abode And soared up to the blissful realms of God." The stone today no longer bears the detail that it once did. In fact, all that remains is a small, illegible square on the ground that has deteriorated quickly over the years. At this rate, there will be nothing left of the stone in another fifty years.

There are many examples of skulls and crossbones throughout the cemetery, and many of the epitaphs include the names of ships and their captains. An incident on July 19, 1794, added eight more graves to the hill. According to the broadside (a single sheet of newspaper that was printed quickly and passed out to the community) printed that day:

An Early Landscape of Death

On Saturday last the following melancholy accident took place in the River Merrimack. As Mr. Chase of Newtown, with eight others, were crossing the River in a small boat, they were unfortunately overtaken by a sudden gust of wind, which overturned the boat, and eight souls were instantly snatched out of time into eternity. Mr. Chase, providentially escaped being drowned, though at great hazard. A solemn warning to youth and the aged!

The broadside went on to say that all eight men were under the age of twenty-nine and that they were decently interred. Below the story was a poem that served as a grim reminder of how fragile life is and that there is nothing to fear in death. It's quite remarkable that the information and the wording in the broadside were so similar to many of the sentiments found on the gravestones in the burial ground.

Alongside the hill is the large Pierce tomb that houses members of the Pierce family who died of tuberculosis between 1863 and 1899. It is immediately evident that the door to the tomb has been resealed in recent years. This tomb has been opened by vandals at least three times since 1925. Vandals first gained entrance to the tomb by digging an opening behind it and breaking through the crumbling stonework. According to records, the youths opened the coffins and removed the clothes from the corpses, put them on and danced around the burial ground. The corpses were also propped up to seated positions, and candles were placed around them. They were then poked with sticks. The vandals were finally reported to the police after being spotted in the decayed clothing, and they confessed to their deed. The clothing was placed back on the corpses, and the tomb was closed up.

In 1985, vandals broke into the same tomb again, this time setting it up as a clubhouse. They brought in alcohol and poured it into the corpses' mouths and took all of the rotting clothing off of them when they observed the alcohol pouring out of the bodies. The caretaker to the grounds found that the tomb had been broken into and alerted the police. The police made a public appeal on the front page of the local newspaper for the vandals to come forward. The vandals confessed and were brought immediately to the hospital to be examined, as the bodies they had disturbed belonged to those who had died from contagious diseases. The three boys did not contract any of the diseases, according to records.

In 2005, a man doing court-ordered community work in the burial ground kicked in the entrance of the Pierce tomb. He twisted a skull off one of the skeletons and posed for pictures with it. He showed the skull to the other community service workers, who ran away upon seeing it. When he was done playing with the skull, he kicked it down the hill, where it was later recovered in an animal hole. Police could not identify the dismembered corpse because the silver nameplates that accompany each body in the crypt had been stolen in the previous break-in. The court sentenced the man to two and a half years in jail for the crime, and the tomb was sealed once more.

People have claimed over the years that the cemetery is haunted and that two ghostly figures can often be seen walking through the door of the Pierce tomb and crossing the burial ground. Some people believe that they have captured infrared photographs of the ghosts walking into the door of the tomb. Many residents believe that the tomb is the center of ghostly activity in the burial ground because of all the vandalism over the years.

Whether you choose to believe in the stories of ghosts or not, Old Hill Burying Ground remains legendary for many reasons.

OLD BURYING GROUND, GROTON

This gravestone in Groton features an hourglass and the words *Hora Fugit*, which means "time flies" in Latin.

Located in Nashoba Valley along the Nashua River in central Massachusetts is the town of Groton. The colonists first arrived in 1655, and they set out building a community that included farms, mills and a meetinghouse. Five garrison houses were constructed as a safe fortress against Native American attacks. An attack on March 13, 1676, emptied the village, and the settlers fled to Concord and Boston until they felt it was safe to return. They had to rebuild most of the town after the Indian raids destroyed everything by fire. Deadly confrontations continued with the natives until 1723.

The Old Burying Ground is located near the site of the

second meetinghouse. Most people were buried where they lived during the early settlement. The oldest gravestone in the cemetery belongs to James Prescott, who died at the age of twenty on May 19, 1704. The grounds of the cemetery are quite hilly due to the underground tombs. In 1872, the town decided to have the tombs uncovered and filled in. Many of the tombs were deemed to be "dilapidated" and needed to be "destroyed." It was suggested that the friends of the deceased could mark the graves with new stones so that their loved ones could be identified.

The cemetery is meticulously maintained and is well marked. The winding paths over the grassy knolls are quite welcoming to the interested visitor. There are a number of unique grave markers with remarkable carvings. An exceptional gravestone is for Jonas Cutler, who died in 1782. The gravestone depicts a large coat of arms and a shield with three wolf heads. Flanking the corners of the stone are two angels, complete with tiny arms that are floating on clouds. The tombstone for Jonathan Clark Lewis, who died in 1781, also has a coat of arms that bears a griffin and three crosses.

The grave of Simeon Ames features a stylized winged skull that is accompanied by an hourglass, two hex symbols and two star-filled circles.

Here lies ye body of Simeon Ames
ye son of Mr. Samuel and Mrs. Hannah Ames
a hopeful an promising young man but cruel death
that regards none snatched him out of the world in
the bloom of life and early frustrated the fond hopes
of his indulgent parents and raised expectation of his
acquaintance he was much beloved in his life and
greatly lamented in his death he died of the smallpox
arborr ye 10th AD 1760 Aged 19 years 5 months and 6 days.
Remember thy Creator in the days of thy youth for this faith
the Lord I Love them that Love me and those that seek me early shall find me.

The monument for Captain Abraham Child reads like a history book or a résumé:

Man lives his little hour and Falls too oft unheeded down

Sacred to the Memory of Capt Abram Child
who was born at Waltham, 1741 and died at Groton, Jan.
3, 1834, Aged 93 yrs. He entered the army in the French
War at the age of 17 yrs. Was with Gen. Amherst at the

capture of Ticonderoga and Crown Point in 1759. He was
a lieutenant among the Minute Men and aided in the Concord
Fight, and the Battle of Bunker Hill in 1775.

Joining Washington, he was one of the Immortal Band which
crossed the Delaware, Dec. 25, 1776,
and turned the tide of war, in the Victories of Trenton and Princeton.
Detached to the North, he fought in the two Battles of Stillwater and
witnessed the surrender of Burgoyne in 1777.
Rejoining Washington, he bore equally the Frosts of Valley
Forge and the Heats of Monmouth in 1778. Detailed with
Gen. Wayne, he crowned his Military career by heading the
Infantry as oldest Captain in the gallant capture of
Stoney Point in 1779, where he received the only wound
that marked his eventful services.

A willow and urn decorate the grave of Lucy Lewis:

Mrs LUCY wife of
Mr Asa Lewis
DIED Sept 29 1835
Aet. 58
Our life how short again a sigh
We live and then begin to die
But oh how great a mercy this
That death's a portal into bliss!
My soul death swallows up thy fears
My grave clothes wipe away all tears
Why should we fear this parting pain
Who die that we may live again.

The inscription on Mary Lakin's grave is very descriptive of how the body decays:

Memento mori

Here lies the Remains of
Miss Mary Lakin the Daughter of
Mr. William Lakin and
Mrs. Miriam his wife

who departed this Life June 3rd 1769
In the 28 year of her age
Corruption earth and worms
Shall but refine her flesh
Till her triumphant Spirit comes
To take it on afresh

Three winged angels can be found on the gravestone for Samuel Bowers, who was a tavern keeper in Groton:

Memento Mori

Here lies Buried the Body of M Samuel Bowers
of who departed this Life
the Sixteenth Day of December Anno Domini
1768 Half a hour after of Three of the
Clock in ye Afternoon and in the
Fifty Eight year Of his age

There are many tall pine trees throughout the burial ground, and crows call to each other over the rustling breeze. The late afternoon is a perfect time to visit the grounds when light and shadow are the best for picture taking. Walking over the hilly terrain leaves one ready to sit down for a while and rest. Why not sit in front of a gravestone and learn one of the stories of the cemetery's permanent residents?

OLD BURIAL HILL, PLYMOUTH

Each slanting gravestone in crowded Old Burial Hill in Plymouth is a solemn reminder of a soul who passed through here lifetimes ago. The hundreds of gravestones yield a collection of stories as old as America itself. The teeming rows of gravestones along disappearing paths appear like sentinels on the hill overlooking Plymouth Harbor. The ground's twisting walkways wind through the trees and down the sloping hillsides. There is a variety of portrait-style stones that feature carved facial expressions, and one can't help wonder how accurate a portrayal these portraits are of those who lie below.

The burial ground is 165 feet above sea level and was an early lookout post for the Pilgrims. The first fort was built on the hill in 1622. It was later modified several times, and after approximately fifty years, the fort was abandoned.

Above: There are so many gravestones at Plymouth's Old Burial Hill Cemetery that it takes more than one visit to see them all.

Left: A very graphic depiction of a skull and crossbones can be found on the gravestone for John Bartlett, who died in 1773.

Sometime around the 1670s, the area was used for burial purposes. A majority of the older stones were made in Britain and shipped across the waters. The oldest surviving tombstone dates from 1681. The stones are a visual connection to some of the most fascinating stories from this old settlement.

One of the most noticeable grave markers is that of Governor William Bradford. The over eight-foot-tall marble obelisk marks the grave of the man who was elected governor of Plymouth Colony thirty times. Born in Austerfield, Yorkshire, England, in March 1588, he was the second signer and primary architect of the Mayflower Compact. He was also an early historian of Plymouth County and is well known for his 270-page journal (later named *History of the Plymouth Plantation*) that chronicles the history of the Pilgrims and the original settlement in Plymouth. During the winter of 1656–57, William Bradford was quite ill, and on May 8, 1657, he predicted to his friends and family that he would die, and he did the next day, at the age of sixty-nine.

Below is a snippet of what is written on this gravestone:

> *Under this stone rest the ashes of William Bradford*
> *a zealous Puritan & sincere Christian Gov.*
> *of Ply. Col. From 1621 to 1657,*
> *(the year he died) aged 69,*
> *except 5 yrs. Which he declined.*

There is a small stone for Caleb Cook, a soldier who killed the infamous King Philip. King Philip was a Wampanoag Indian leader who led the uprising against the New England colonists known as King Philip's War. These raids were proportionately some of the bloodiest and costliest in the history of America. More than half of New England's ninety towns—including Deerfield, Haverhill, Northfield, Bridgewater, Scituate and Northampton—were assaulted by Native American warriors in the seventeenth century. While in battle at Providence, Rhode Island, Caleb, after an initial misfire, shot King Philip directly in the heart. After the fatal shot, Caleb ran out of the bushes to switch his gun out for King Philip's. This gun was a treasured heirloom that was passed down in the Cook family for hundreds of years. King Philip's body was drawn and quartered and his limbs hung from the trees. His decapitated head was brought back to Plymouth, where it was put on a stake and displayed for over thirty years.

There is the local legend of a witch known as Mother Crewe whom many believed was responsible for sending several people to their graves at Old Burial Hill. Mother Crewe was avoided by many people in town, whether or not they believed in witchcraft. She was thought to be responsible for causing seemingly healthy plants and crops to rot the vine. She was accused of driving ships sailing along the coast to shore. There was even a story about her causing villagers to be stricken with smallpox.

One of the most famous stories about Mother Crewe describes an encounter she had with another Plymouth resident named Southland Howland. According to the story, Howland one day rode up to Mother Crewe's door and attempted to seize her property, as he felt that he was the rightful owner. Howland demanded that she give up her home to him under the law of entail (a common law at that time that restricted the sale of property, protecting the inheritance of the heirs). With a snap of his whip upon Mother Crewe's door, Howland laid claim to the property. When she stood firm and told him that he had no rights to the claim, he told her that he would "tear down" her cabin by the next Friday. "On Friday they'll dig your grave on Burying Hill. I see the shadow closing round you. You draw it in with every breath. Quick! Home and make your peace!" she replied.

The exchange continued between Howland and the old witch. "Bandy," he said. "No witch words with me, woman. On Friday I will return." With that, he swung himself onto his horse. All of a sudden, a black cat jumped onto Mother Crewe's shoulder, hissing. She raised her hand and cried, "Your day is near its end. Repent!"

Howland's last words to her were, "Bah! You have heard what I have said. If on Friday you are not elsewhere, I'll tear the timbers down and bury you in the ruins."

"Enough!" shrieked the hag. "My curse is on you here and hereafter. Die! Then go down to hell!" Mother Crewe's cat jumped on the horse, clawing at him, and the horse ran off wildly.

A sinister fog encircled the town that brought a cold gloom. Just before dark, the dead body of Howland was found lying on the ground, not far from Mother Crewe's house. Southland Howland's sudden death was unexplained and remains a mystery. Was it just happenstance that his corpse was buried on the Friday he was supposed to return on Old Burial Hill?

Mother Crewe's curses were believed to be the reason for other burials on the hill. In the book *Dr. Le Baron and His Daughters* (1890), author Jane G. Austin describes Mother Crewe issuing a deadly curse:

> But mother Crewe's face showed no sign of
> relenting as she gazed upon that trembling figure,
> decked out with its poor attempt at bridal finery; indeed,
> an added scorn and detestation seemed to gather

upon her brow, and, bending over the girl, her arms
stiffly extended upward, she deliberately cursed her in
all the detail of anathema to be gathered from the black
and bitter pages of wizard lore: sleeping, waking, in her
home and among her neighbors, in her body and in her
soul, in her life and in her death, and in a dishonored
grave. "And may your husband fail in all he undertakes
and die of a broken heart, and may all your
sons be cripples, and all your girls lighted and deserted
as mine has been, and no one to pity or to help"

Yet another curse of Mother Crewe's concerned a story of a young sailor named Ansel Ring. Ansel was on the ill-fated, armed brigantine the *General Arnold*, which was under the command of Captain James Magee of Boston in 1778. A terrible blizzard blew into Plymouth harbor the day after Christmas. In danger, the ship dropped anchor and was hung up in an area known as White Flats, a treacherous sandbar just northwest of the breakwater.

Fierce waves pummeled the ship, and the bitter winter temperatures dropped below zero. Captain Magee told the crewmen to put rum in their shoes to ward off frostbite, but many drank it instead and died quickly after. In a blinding snowstorm, the crew desperately tried to survive the night. Their screams through the wailing winds could be heard across the water in the settlement. The frosty morning light revealed seventy-two bodies that were frozen to death and strewn about the ship. Dr. Thatcher, a Plymouth native, viewed the horrible discovery and chronicled the account:

Seventy dead bodies, frozen into all imaginable postures, were strewed over the deck, or attached to the shrouds and spars; about thirty exhibited signs of life, but were unconscious whether in life or death. The bodies remained in the posture in which they died; the features dreadfully distorted. Some were erect, some bending forward, some sitting with the head resting on the knees, and some with both arms extended, clinging to spars or some parts of the vessel.

The dead were piled on the floor of the Court House in town, and it is said that Dr. Robbins fainted when called to perform the religious services.

On Old Burial Hill, a mass grave was dug for those who died on the ship. There was no complete list of names of those onboard. Many of the voyagers had been picked up in Boston before the brig set sail, and they hadn't been on board long enough for the captain to log their identities. The tragedy cast a dark shadow on Plymouth that year. The townspeople who witnessed the horrific scene and heard the screams wanted to forget but couldn't. Years passed, and the tale became lost to time. Alongside one of the many pathways in the cemetery is the monument that serves as a reminder of those dark days. Ansel Ring, who froze to death on the ship, is also buried here. Additionally, there is a stone on the hill that marks the grave of Hannah Howland, who died "of a languishment" on January 25, 1780. Hannah is said to have died of a broken heart because of the passing her lover, Ansel. Perhaps Mother Crewe's curse had come to pass.

The monument marking the grave of the sailors of the *General Arnold* can be found at the far edge of the burial ground, near the Russell Street parking lot. The inscription on the northeastern side reads:

In memory of Seventy two Seamen who perished in Plymouth arbor
on the 26, and 27, days of December 1778,
on board the private armed Brig, Gen. Arnold, of twenty guns,
James Magee of Boston, Commander, sixty of whom were buried on
this spot.

On the northwestern side, the monument reads: "Capt. James Magee died in Roxbury, February 4, 1801; aged 51 years." And there is a small bit of text on the southwestern side:

Oh! Falsely flattering were yon billows smooth
When forth, elated, sailed in evil hour,
That vessel whose disastrous fate, when told,
Fill'd every breast with sorrow and each eye
With piteous tears.

Finally, there is a dedication on the southeastern side:

This monument marks the resting place of sixty of the seventy two mariners,
"who perished in their strife with the storm," and is erected by Stephen
Gale of Portland, Maine, a stranger to them, as a just memorial of their
sufferings and death.

Locals tell tales of a ghost ship that they believe to be the *General Arnold*, complete with a phantom crew. The ship is said to sail the harbor and disappears into the mist when approached by other ships. It's also said that one of the best places to view this ghost ship is from Old Burial Hill.

Numerous stones for shipwrecks and those lost at sea can be found in Old Burial Hill, and many of them bear remarkable carvings. There is the gravestone for Captain Chandler Holmes, who died October 4, 1831, at the age of twenty-seven. On the stone is an image of a sinking ship in the ocean, and there is a trumpeting angel flying above it. The grave of Richard Holmes—who was drowned in the Pacific Ocean near the port of Lima, Peru, and died at the age of twenty-two—features a dramatic carving of an angel trumpeting over a floating coffin. Lightning, bands of rain and waves washing over a ship's decks are engraved on the stone for Joseph Churchill, who died at the age of fifty-four while aboard the brigantine *Plymouth Rock*. The ship foundered at sea in November 1836 while en route to Rochelle, France. The same stone tells the story of his son, who also went to a watery grave. Captain Joseph Lewis of Portland, Maine, at the age of thirty-seven, died on the brigantine *Androscoggin* in August 1842.

There are quite a large number of portrait stones throughout the burial ground. Some of the carvings for women depict them being adorned with necklaces that have hearts on them. A fascinating carving on Nathaniel Morton's grave depicts a well-dressed man wearing a wig rising from behind a grave marked with two skulls and crossbones.

There's a building close to the cemetery that is rumored to be haunted by the spirits of the interred. The top floor was used by medical students who dissected fresh bodies that they obtained from Old Burial Hill. Old Burial Hill itself is not without its ghostly legends as well. With all of the fantastic carvings and tragic tales, it's not surprising that the spirits are active. Visitors to the burial ground have claimed to have seen shadow people wandering the grounds, sometimes walking between the trees, as if the ghosts of the past were still keeping watch on the hill. There is an unsettling story of a group of five people who wandered between the stones on a gloomy November evening. The five stopped to talk but then heard loud footsteps coming up the sidewalk directly toward them. The group frantically searched for the source of the sound but found nothing. They quickly found the nearest exit and made a hasty retreat and were in complete disbelief of what had transpired. Tour groups regularly walk the well-trod paths, and many have reported capturing mysterious light anomalies, orbs and other unexplainable phenomena on camera.

Another burial site in town worth noting is on Cole's Hill, which offers a sweeping view of the bay. At the foot of Cole's Hill is Plymouth Rock, the legendary landing site of the Pilgrims and steppingstone to the New World. On the hill, there is a statue of Massasoit that bears the following inscription: "Great Sachem of The Wampanoags Protector and Preserver of the pilgrims 1621, Erected by the Improved Order of Red Men as a Grateful Tribute 1921." Nearby is a sarcophagus that contains the bones of the Pilgrims that have been found at various times near its location. The sarcophagus was erected by the General Society of Mayflower Descendants in 1920. A part of the inscription reads:

> *The Monument marks the First Burying Ground in Plymouth of the passengers of the Mayflower. Here under cover of darkness the fast dwindling company laid their dead, leveling the earth above them lest the Indians should know how many were the graves.*

In the book *The Pilgrim Republic* (1879), John A. Goodwin describes how the remains of the interred at Cole's Hill were unearthed:

> *In a storm of 1735 a torrent pouring down Middle Street made a ravine in Cole's Hill and washed many human remains down into the harbor. In 1809 a skull with especially fine teeth was exposed. In 1855 these graves were exposed in laying the public conduit on Cole's Hill. In one grave lay two skeletons, pronounced by surgeons male and female. The man had a particularly noble forehead; and it was fondly surmised that here were the remains of Mr. and Mrs. Carver. These found a new grave on Burial Hill; but the other relics, with barbaric taste, were placed in the top of the stone canopy over Forefathers' Rock. In 1879, during some work on the southeast side of the hill, many more bones were unearthed, and some, with questionable taste, were carried away by the spectators in remembrance of their renowned sires.*

Plymouth is a resting place for the brave men who settled an unknown land and suffered and struggled to shepherd the beginnings of what became a free nation. Perhaps their spirits look out over the hills of this deep-rooted town and still keep watch over the rolling waves of the harbor.

OLD DEERFIELD BURYING GROUND
(OLD ALBANY CEMETERY)

It is said that burying the dead is a part of life. Located in picturesque western Massachusetts is the village of Old Deerfield. First settled by European colonists in 1673, this settlement is a collection of eighteenth- and nineteenth-century houses that are filled with relics of hearth and home, which emphasize the intimate details of life in early New England. When English traders first saw Deerfield, in the 1640s, it was inhabited by the Pocumtucks, a small but prosperous and powerful group of Indians who had lived, farmed, fished and hunted in the area for several generations.

At the beginning of the eighteenth century, Deerfield was only one of a few settlements in western New England. The settlement was seen as quite a threat to the Native Americans as the settlers were slowly expanding and claiming more and more land. The French also had an interest in trying to stop the growth of the English empire in the New World. On a cold winter morning in February 1704, 340 French soldiers and Indians swarmed over the frozen snow and raided the settlement, taking 112 Deerfield men, women and children captive and marching them three hundred miles to Montreal, Canada, in harsh winter conditions. The long, snowy trek claimed many lives. Some people starved to death, and others who couldn't keep up were hacked into pieces by the Indians. Some of the captives were later redeemed and returned to Deerfield, but one-third chose to remain among their French and native captors. Many of the Deerfield villagers were sold by the Indians to the French, who later ransomed them back to the British.

Deerfield was resettled in 1707 under the leadership of the town's first minister, Reverend John Williams. Reverend Williams had managed to survive the raid of 1704 and the long march to Canada. He was also held captive by the French for two years, and he lost his wife and two of his children during that time. Eunice, the reverend's third child, married a Mohawk and chose to remain with the Indians and French until her death in 1785.

The stones in the old burial ground of Deerfield village date back to the 1690s, and some of the graves are from the 1800s. It is believed that the site may have been a Native American burial ground at an earlier time. There is a four-foot-tall grassy mound that marks a mass grave in the graveyard. On the summit of the mound is a stone that is inscribed on one face: "The Dead of 1704." And on the opposite side of the mound, a stone reads, "The Grave of 48 Men Women and Children, victims of the French and Indian raid on Deerfield February 29, 1704." The marker was placed there in 1901 to commemorate those who were killed in the Deerfield massacre.

The Memorial Hall museum in Deerfield has a collection of fascinating artifacts from the 1704 raid, including a door from what is known as the Old Indian House, which is also known as the Ensign John Sheldon House. The door retains the hole and gashes that were made by French and Indian attackers. Also in the hall are marble tablets that describe the lives of many of those who were affected by the raid and some that memorialize those who are buried in the old burial ground:

In honor of the Pioneers
of this Valley, by whose courage
and energy, faith and fortitude
the savage was expelled
and the wilderness subdued;
and to perpetuate the remembrance
of the sufferings at Deerfield,
FEB. *29, 1703–4,*
when, before the break of day, 340 French and Indians,
under the Sieur Hertel de Rouville,
swarming in over the palisades on the drifted snow,
surprised and sacked the sleeping town,
and killed or captured
the greater part of its inhabitants.

On Tablets at either hand,
recorded in love and reverence by their kindred;
are the names and ages of those
who lost their lives in the assault,
or were slain on the meadows
in the heroic attempt to rescue the captives,
or who died on the hurried retreat to Canada,
victims to starvation

SARAH FIELD, 2.
MARY, her mother, 28,
Wife of JOHN,
With children,
MARY, 6, and JOHN, 3,
were captured.
Mary adopted by an Indian,
Was named WALAHOWEY.
She married a savage,
and became one.

Zechariah Field
1645–674.
A settler at Pocumtuck
Before Philip's war.
His remains lie in an unknown grave

In the old burying ground.
Many of his descendants
Have attained international fame.
In his honor
This tablet is placed in 1903
by Marshall Field
of Chicago.
In Memory
of
Mr. Samuel Allen,
who was killed by the Indians on the meadow north of
The Bars Homestead
while valiantly defending his children,
August 25, 1746:
of Eunice Allen,
his daughter, aged 13, who was tomahawked by the Indians,
but survived:
of Samuel Allen,
his son, aged 8, who was taken captive by the Indians,
but after many months was rescued through the
gratitude of an Indian woman, by his uncle,
Col. John Hawks.
Both children thus restored to their mother,
Hannah Hawks Allen,
lived to be the oral historians of this eventful day
and of their generation.
Erected by the descendants of
Caleb Allen,
son of Mr. Samuel Allen of "The Bars"

Many of the early gravestones in the tranquil burial ground refer directly to the horrors of the Indian attacks.

Metal rivets hold together the stone for Lieutenant Mehuman Hinsdell, and a skull and crossbones are carved at the top of the stone. The inscription reads:

Here Lyes Buried the body of
Lievt Mehuman Hinsdell
Decd May Ye 9th 1736
In the 65th Year of his age
was the first male child

born in this place and was
twice captivated by the indian salvages

It is believed that the gravestone for Judah Wright was commissioned after his death and was actually carved in Dorchester, Massachusetts, by James Foster. A winged angel is depicted on the stone, which bears the following inscription:

In Memory of Mr. Judah Wright
who died August 30th, 1747
In the 72d year of his Age
He was one of the unfortunate persons
who was captured by the Indians February 29th 1703–1704

There are several other stories in the old burial ground behind Deerfield Academy. A dramatic carving can be found on the gravestone for Mary Harvey. It was carved by Solomon Ashley, a misfit son of the town minister who had never married. Solomon had become a common potter and gravestone maker, and he eventually became a ward of the town. He drowned at the age of sixty-nine.

Mary's husband was Simeon Harvey, the village blacksmith. Simeon was born in 1743 and was apprenticed to the trade in 1761 after a brief service in the army. In 1768, he married Mary, and one year later, they had their first child. Every two years thereafter, another child was born into the family. However, in 1785, just five days before Christmas and just before Mary and

Carved by Solomon Ashley, the gravestone for Mary Harvey features an image of a woman inside a coffin with an infant in her left arm.

Simeon's eighteenth wedding anniversary, Mary died giving birth to their tenth child. The gravestone for Mary is engraved with a simple carving of an open coffin and depicts Mary with her infant lying in her left arm, just as they were buried. This depiction of the deceased was quite unusual for the time.

The stone for Abagail Williams, who died in 1754, features a rare design of a large clock with roman numerals, crossed bones and a crossed shovel and pickaxe.

There are also several table stones in the burial ground that are on the verge of falling apart. Table stones were used to elevate the deceased above others in the burial ground and were usually for members of the clergy and military and sometimes doctors. In the early 1900s, it was said that local boys used to use the table stones to crack the nuts from the nearby trees, which may have contributed to the condition of these fragile stones.

Funerary expenses were costly, and oftentimes, simple fieldstone markers were placed on the graves. Sometimes friends or family members would take a stone right off of their own property and try their hand at scratching an inscription on the rock. Fieldstone markers are sometimes not marked and are easily overlooked in a graveyard. There are a handful of fieldstone markers in the Old Deerfield Burying Ground. A carving on a small, red fieldstone marker for Mercy Allen, who died at the age of one, plainly reads: " MA Dyed Novem 7 Anno 1696."

The rough fieldstone marker for Daniel Belding bears the inscription:

danl beld
in dyed
jvne ye 1
at 10 movnths
ovld 1730 and
danl in ienry ye
1 1731 an inf-
ant danls
sons

Other stones list the cause of death, such as smallpox, which was a common cause of death in 1785. A stone from 1793 reads, "As a tribute of gratitude to the memory of an indulgent stepmother." Another marker from 1804 bears this puzzling epitaph: "Your eyes are upon me, and I am not."

The gravestone for Rebecca Arms tells the detailed story of her death. According to records, she was crushed by an avalanche of grain during a house fire.

On the 12th Day of May 1768,
the Home of Mr. William Arms was
Consumed by Fire And his
Wife Mrs. Rebecca Arms unhappily perished in the
Flames in the 70th year of her Age.

She was one who Feared God & Lov'd the Redeemer,
was a singular Example of Piety,
who by a devout walk was a Bright
Or name to the Christian Religion,
And her Death Great Gain.

Every year around the anniversary of the raid, colonial reenactors commemorate the events of 1704, and some of the stories of those buried in the burial ground are retold. A visit to the burial ground at any time of the year shows a glimpse into the past of those who lived in a frontier wilderness. The memory of those settlers who survived the assault and came back to rebuild the ruins of Deerfield lives on within the burial ground's stone walls.

UNION STREET CEMETERY (MEADOW CEMETERY), WEST SPRINGFIELD

Located in a busy area of West Springfield (in a village that was once known as Cold Spring) is the Union Street Cemetery, which is sometimes referred to as Meadow Cemetery. The cemetery was officially established in 1711, although it is speculated that burials may have taken place a few years before 1711. Although settlers had been living in the area since 1654, they were required to bury their dead on the east side of the "Great River" (Connecticut River) for the first fifty years of their settlement. The funeral processions across the river were oftentimes difficult for the families and added more pressure for the grieving mourners.

The cemetery was used for about one hundred years, and it is an easy burial ground to wander about, as it is only about an acre in size. Most of the stones are made from sandstone, which was used frequently in some areas of the Connecticut River valley. There are many simple fieldstone markers with only names and years carved on them. The gravestone for Martha Ely is marked 1702 and is the oldest stone on the grounds. Martha was originally buried on the east side of the Connecticut River, and she was reinterred in the Union Street Cemetery after 1711.

The stone carver changed the month from October to November on the stone for John Day.

A very unusual gravestone with a double portrait can be found in Meadow Cemetery in Springfield.

While some of the red sandstone gravestones in the cemetery are crumbling, there are many that are in good condition.

Toward the center of the cemetery is a tall brownstone obelisk that was erected for the town's first minister, Reverend John Woodbridge, who died from the fall of a tree branch in 1718. He was much beloved by the community, and the decision was made to build an obelisk in 1852, as his original gravestone had deteriorated. The monument reads:

Rev. John Woodbridge
First minister of West Springfield after
Serving his generation faithfully
Fell asleep June 10, 1718

The righteous shall be of everlasting remembrance

Erected by the descendents of his parishioners in 1852.

Also featured on the 1852 monument are the names of many of the first settlers of the town who are buried on the grounds.

A gravestone for Nathaniel Dwight (the stone reads Dwit) displays an interesting carved skull and rosettes on the border. He was from Northampton, and he was visiting West Springfield when he died. Nathaniel was the first person to be buried in the cemetery after the land was donated to the town by Edward and Sarah Foster in 1711.

The gravestone for Ebenezer Day, who died in 1763 at the age of eighty-six, displays a droopy-eyed angel that bears a "crown of righteousness," which was carved by Joseph Williston. The only table stones that exist in West Springfield can be found in the cemetery and are for the Mirick family. It's unusual for families to have these large stones, as they are quite expensive, sometimes costing five times more than a standard gravestone. Sadly, the stones have deteriorated and broken over the years.

There are several fascinating epitaphs in the cemetery that illustrate eighteenth-century attitudes toward death. The stones for John Day and Ithamer Ward display corrections of dates and names by the gravestone carver. The gravestone for Richard Ely features an angel with a missing nose, as indicated by the rectangle carved out of the face. It was carved by Nathaniel Phelps. The nose was carefully cut out to be corrected, but somewhere along the line, the replacement went missing. Oddly, there are other stones in the Pioneer Valley with angels missing noses that were also carved by Nathaniel Phelps.

The grave of John Andrew Insense tells part of the story of his life:

> *In Memory of John Andrew Insense born in*
> *Little Biwene, was a dragoon in the Prince of Brunswicks Regt who was*
> *killed by lightning August 16th 1780 in the 28th year of his age*
> *"Ich weis Dasmein Ertoeser Leptund, er wird Mich wieder*
> *Dus der Auferwecken" Job Capt 19th 25th*

Insense was one of the Hessian mercenaries who were hired by the British to fight against the colonists during the Revolutionary War. In 1777, he was taken prisoner after Burgoyne's surrender in Saratoga and then he was forced to march in a blinding snowstorm to Boston. Insense and several other soldiers deserted the troops in West Springfield and settled there.

In 1850, Thomas Bridgman from Northampton recounted Insense's death: "Joseph and Tilley Merrick were under the tree when it was struck with Lightning; they were both knocked down. Deacon Joseph Merrick remained speechless for several days...Insense was some 20 feet from the tree, when he was killed, having taken shelter from the storm under a cock of hay."

One of the most unusual gravestones in western Massachusetts is a tall gravestone featuring the carved portraits of Hezekiah and Mary Day. The detail is quite remarkable, and the dramatic inscription reads:

In Memory of Mr Hezekiah Day
Who died Octr 11th 1778
In the 78th year of his age
Also Mrs. Mary his wife
Who died August 7th, 1780
In the 71st year of her age.
Life's uncertain Death is sure
Sins the wound And Christ the cure

The cemetery provides visitors with a glimpse of eighteenth-century history and imparts the beliefs of the people of West Springfield. While all of the cemeteries in the town are owned by churches or private associations, Union Cemetery is the only one owned and maintained by the Town of West Springfield.

HANCOCK CEMETERY, QUINCY

Located in Quincy Square, across from the First Parish Church, is historic Hancock Cemetery, named after the Reverend John Hancock, who was the father of the famous John Hancock. One of the country's oldest burial grounds, the cemetery was founded sometime in the 1630s and was the town's main burial ground until 1854. In 1809, a group of citizens including John Adams purchased the grounds and donated it to the town. It was established at that point the "town shall never hereafter allow the said burial ground to be used as a pasture or any horse or cattle to run at large therein."

Many of the gravestones refer to the town of "Braintree" or "Braintry," and in 1792, the town split off into sections, and the center became Quincy. The oldest gravestone belongs to Reverend William Tompson, the first minister in the town, and is dated 1666. The use of burial tombs began in 1675 with the tomb of Dr. Leonard Hoar, who was the third president of Harvard College. One of the tombs is known as the minister's tomb and is the final resting place for Reverend John Hancock and many of the other early ministers in the town's history.

There are several rows of underground tombs that surround all four sides of the cemetery as well, and the most famous of them is the Adams tomb. The tomb was the burial site of President John Adams and President John Quincy Adams before they and their wives were moved across the street to tombs in the basement of the United First Parish Church. Built in 1828 and funded by John Adams himself, the church is made from Quincy granite and is sometimes referred to as the president's church.

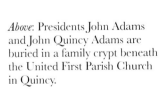

Above: Presidents John Adams and John Quincy Adams are buried in a family crypt beneath the United First Parish Church in Quincy.

Right: The original burial tomb for John Quincy Adams is located right across the street from the United First Parish Church.

The beautiful gate for the Hancock Cemetery in Quincy features funerary urns.

Lieutenant John Cleverly, who died in 1703, has one of the cemetery's most notable gravestones. The gravestone was carved by Boston stone carver John Noyes and is the earliest in New England to have birds carved on it; this went on to be a common theme. The birds are thought to represent phoenixes (which represented immortality) or peacocks (which represented incorruptibility).

The inscription on the memorial gravestone for Henry Adams describes the history of the man who was the great-great-grandfather of John Adams, who died in 1646:

> *In Memory of HENRY ADAMS who took his flight from the Dragon* [sic] *persecution in Devonshire in England, and alighted with eight sons, near Mount Wollaston. One of the sons returned to England, and after taking time to explore the country, four removed to Medfield and the neighboring towns; two to Chelmsford. One only, Joseph, who lies here at his left hand, remained here, who was an original proprietor in the township of Braintree, incorporated in 1639. This stone and several others have been placed in this yard, by a great-great grandson, from a veneration of the Piety, humility, simplicity, prudence, patience, temperance, frugality, industry and perseverance, of his Ancestors, in hopes of Recommending an imitation of their virtues to their posterity. Erected December, 1823.*

The dramatic iron gates and fencing that surround the cemetery were constructed in 1844, and the top of the fence features funerary urns as finials. The cemetery is well maintained and was placed on the National Register of

Historic Places in 1982. The First Parish Church across the street offers tours of the burial chamber where both of the Adamses are interred. They also offer tourist maps of Hancock Cemetery at the end of the tour.

OLD BURYING GROUND, CAMBRIDGE

The city of Cambridge was known as Newtowne until 1638, and the town's original cemetery was somewhere along Brattle Street. It was deemed that the cemetery was not safe from the intrusions of wild animals, and the cemetery was not used after 1634. There is no indication of where the cemetery is in the city today, as it has been lost to time and urban development. The city was set out in a grid-like system, and the families worked planting the fields, each with a share of the common land.

The Old Burying Ground was established around 1635 and was originally about an acre in size, but when the Cambridge Common was enclosed, the size doubled. In 1760, the Christ Church was constructed, and the western boundary of the cemetery was established. The First Parish Church was built in 1833, near the eastern side of the cemetery. The cemetery served the city for nearly two hundred years as the final resting place for a variety of people, from the paupers to the wealthy elite. There are 1,218 known graves on the grounds, but it is believed that there are hundreds more interred in the cemetery, as many of the original graves remain unmarked.

There are several table stones for some of the wealthiest residents who are buried in the cemetery; other people of status chose to be buried in

Death imps carrying death darts can be found in the Old Burying Ground in Cambridge.

The gravestone for Samuel Bridge dates back to 1672, making it more than 325 years old.

underground tombs. One of the most elaborate tombs is for Colonel John Vassall, who died in 1747. He was a Harvard graduate and was part of the Massachusetts militia. The tomb was opened in 1862, and it contained twenty-five caskets. One of the people interred in the tomb was Andrew Craigie, who had acquired the family's Christ Church pew and burial plot, along with the Vassal estate in 1792.

There are at least nineteen Revolutionary War soldiers buried in the cemetery, as well as eight Harvard College presidents. Several African Americans are also buried in the Old Burying Ground. By 1811, the cemetery had become full, with the exception of the tombs, and the cemetery was no longer used. A new iron fence was built sometime before 1891, and in 1900, many of the old headstones were repaired and reset. Trees were also planted around the same time.

One of the most notable gravestones in the cemetery is William Dickson's, dated 1692. The carving portrays two death imps, each carrying a "death dart" and an hourglass along the borders of the stone. Evil demons of death were some of the symbols used by Charlestown gravestone carver Joseph Lamson. Imps carrying coffins away are also depicted on the stone. This type of imagery never became popular, as there was no interest in demons or medieval art on gravestones; in fact, such imagery wasn't used after 1710, which makes stones bearing such designs rather unique.

The restoration of Old Burying Ground has been a continual effort, and the most extensive work was done between 1934 and 1976. Cambridge Historical Commission has also restored many grave markers, and its work continues on a regular basis. The cemetery has become a local tourist attraction and brings in visitors from all around the world.

Chapter Three

Dead on the Tide

Cape Cod and the Islands

Come out and play! The laughing, witching spirit of the Cape Cod land calls you. A strange uneasiness creeps into your mood and fleeting pictures of sky and water and cloud flit before your eyes. A breeze stirs your papers and you know the Spirit of the Cape is there again waving her hand at you through the open window.
—Cape Cod Magazine, *1915*

Cape Cod and the islands of Martha's Vineyard and Nantucket are a unique landscape in Massachusetts. The peninsula is ever changing, growing and shrinking with the threat of erosion that may some day claim the summer vacation paradise. But the roots of superstition run deep here. Hundreds of tales of shipwrecks and seafaring disasters have piled up like shells on this coastline. For many years in the mid-1800s, based on a number of accounts, there was at least one shipwreck each week on the Cape. Despite the sometimes harsh and unbearable conditions that some of the people faced on the Cape, there was no place that many of them would rather be—even in death.

SANDWICH OLD BURIAL GROUND (OLD TOWN CEMETERY), SANDWICH

One of the oldest cemeteries on Cape Cod is the Sandwich Old Burial Ground, which is located right in Sandwich Village. Sandwich, founded in 1637, is the oldest town on the Cape. Some reports say the village's first burial took place in 1639; others list 1663. The headstones document the lives of most of Sandwich's earliest families. Many of the families in the cemetery are

A simple death's head can be found on the grave for John Lewis in Yarmouth.

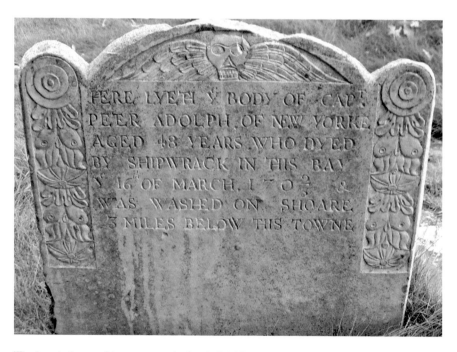

The inscription on this gravestone in Sandwich Village Cemetery describes a body being found after a ship wrecked three miles south of the town.

Protestant, but there a few very interesting Roman Catholic graves to be found as well.

There are many gravestones from the 1600s, and the oldest one dates back to 1683. It belongs to Thomas Clark, who was just seven weeks old when he died. A vast majority of the stones in the burial ground were carved in Boston, although some were carved in Plymouth, Massachusetts, and Newport, Rhode Island.

Here are a few of the many interesting inscriptions found on these headstones:

here lyeth ye body
of shearjashub bourn
esq'r who departed this
life march ye 7th 1718/19
in the 76 year of his age

he was a virtuous righteous & merciful man
and a great friend to ye indians
precious in ye sight of ye lord
is ye death of this saint

A crumbling table stone bears the following inscription:

Here mouldering lies the
Reverend Benjamin Fessenden
who was born at Cambridge June 3d
1701 graduated at Harvard College
ordained minister at Sandwich
June 12th 1722 and deceased
Aug 7th 1746 Age 45. Concerning whom it may
with truth be said that he was an instance of early piety,
and in his youth made swift advances in valuable knowledge;
that, having used his best endeavors
to prepare himself for the service of the Sanctuary,
he was introduced into it with general approbation,
and employed in it to the good of others and his own comfort;
that not only as a divine he was useful,
but as a discreet and successful physician,
and that, after a long exercise of fortitude, readiness
and patience under weakness and various bodily infirmities,
he gave up the ghost with tranquility,
and rests from his trouble and labours

There is a pond near the back of the burial ground that offers a view of the village and all of the historic homes that are across from the cemetery. Beneath the pond's surface are several gravestone bases, which is unfortunate because the gravestones are deteriorating quickly in the cemetery. Some stones are still legible; the writing on those that were transcribed by historians one hundred years ago is barely visible. The cemetery is definitely worth stopping by while in Cape Cod, as it offers a look at the local history of the people, places and events that have faded into memory.

BURIAL OF THE WIDOWS OF CAPE COD

No poorhouses existed in the early days of the Cape Cod Colony. When land that belonged to men who had died could not be sustained by their families, it was disposed of by the order of the General Court, and the "relicts" (widows) would be sold off. The annual process of selling bereaved wives became known as the "widows' vandue." They were sold for what was deemed as a "widdow's yeare" and were often sold more than once. Prices varied yearly, but in 1770, the average value of a widow was three pounds. As the women grew older and more feeble, they were not valued as much, and some towns had difficulty "disposing" of them. Some women were reduced to as low as nine pence per annum, whereas a young, vibrant widow could bring over ten pounds. The expenses of keeping an ill widow always brought about much discussion, as the community didn't feel that it was their responsibility to pay the doctor of the family who had purchased the widow's "charge." Oftentimes, the townspeople argued that the family overworked and underfed her. Such expenses were usually determined in advance, and if those expenses were deemed to be excessive or unnecessary, the widow was forced to continue her service without further medical attention.

It was written that an attractive widow had a good chance of being remarried within the year to a well-off widower, for both men and women at this time believed it wise to console themselves as promptly as possible after a marital loss. Even women from wealthy backgrounds would, surprisingly enough, have to endure the humiliation of a public auction. In 1776, a woman known as Mistress Lovell was set up for one year to Josiah Stevens for the sum of nine pounds and six shillings. She was auctioned eight more times over the following years, and each year, she reportedly grew less and less appealing. According to an account, her clothes were incredibly shabby, so much so that, by 1782, she was in desperate need of a new shirt. The townspeople voted to purchase one for her, and she was sold into service again soon after. This gentle woman spent seven years in servitude and died on a stormy night in September 1783. Her body was put in a "poverty box" (used to bury those who did not have the means to purchase a coffin) and was laid under the pine trees near a local church. Her clothes were deemed unsuitable for her last entrance into the meetinghouse. A sail-cloth was thrown over the coffin while the townspeople debated what to do with her. Finally, they decided that a sheet would be purchased for the widow to be buried in.

There's an extraordinary story that involves Jane Bumpus, a widow of Sieur Louis Bumpasse, who came from France to the French colony in Canada and then migrated south. After her husband died, she was placed for auction, and when she was brought before the townspeople, she scowled and yelled out, "For shame!" The minister instructed Jane to be quiet, and since she was a religious woman, she respected his wishes. Widow Bumpus came from hearty stock and seemed to take care of herself. She was sold to several different families over the years, but each year, she was sold at a lower price and forced to work even harder.

The widow was devoted to the children of these families and also to the ones who lived in the communities in which she served. When diseases like smallpox and diphtheria ran through the community, she would dismiss herself from her contracted service and go and nurse the suffering children. She put little value on her own existence, and her dedication to these children won her their devotion. In fact, many of them called her Aunt Jane.

Smart and outspoken, she kept an eye on the townspeople, too, and she had no problems calling people out when she saw them breaking laws such as not keeping the Sabbath. During town meetings, the widow would show up and detail what had witnessed, and then she would point out the offender. She made many enemies this way, and many continued to despise her even after she died. The vote came down that only a clean shift would be provided for her burial, with no white sheet to wrap her in. To add insult to injury, there was no formal announcement of her funeral. Only the minister showed up to the church to read services over her dead body. But when it was time to nail the coffin shut, the minster was shocked to find that it was completely empty! Further investigation revealed that four of the children (all of whom were under the age of sixteen) whom the widow had nursed back to health were responsible; they had retrieved Jane's body and tenderly placed it in an oak coffin that they had carved by hand. The young men carried the widow's coffin into the woods and gave it a proper burial. They covered her grave with fresh pine boughs and flowers. A handmade cross that was placed there reads:

Mistress Jean Bumpus
Wife of Sir Bumpus of France

A HEART FOR HISTORY, NANTUCKET

One of the most interesting authors when it comes to New England's legends and lore is Edward Rowe Snow. He spent his lifetime studying the lighthouses, islands and legends of the New England coast and chronicled his explorations in a series of books. He was friend to many lighthouse keepers and was also known as the Flying Santa who delivered Christmas presents to the keepers and their families all over New England. He was also a respected lecturer and often brought along unusual treasures—what he called his "traveling museum"—to share with his listeners. Edward Rowe Snow lived a fascinating life, which sadly ended in 1982. He passed away at the age of eighty and was interred in Marshfield Hills Cemetery in Marshfield, Massachusetts.

One of the most interesting tales that he chronicled involved the burial of a heart that belonged to a man named Charles F. Winslow. While browsing through a second-hand bookstore in Boston in 1934, he came across a book that mentioned this unusual interment at South Burial Ground. Edward was more than intrigued, but unfortunately, he didn't have the fifty cents to purchase the book, so he committed the title to memory. (For those interested, the book title is *Island of Nantucket*.) A year later Edward visited Nantucket Island and made a trip to South Burial Ground, but he couldn't find anything in relation to the story that had intrigued him so much. He asked around, but no one seemed to know anything regarding the tale.

Edward came back to the island of Nantucket in 1946 to give a historic lecture. He was the guest of Dr. Will Gardner, and one day while the two men were in Dr. Gardner's study, the subject of Dr. Winslow's heart came up. Before he knew it, Edward was holding a copy of the book he had seen in the bookstore years before. Edward found the page and the passage that had been stuck in his mind all those years.

The very next morning, Dr. Gardner took Edward to South Burial Ground and pointed out the area where the heart was supposedly buried. Even though it was a blustery, rainy day, Edward was determined to find the grave of Dr. Winslow, and after searching for a while, he found it. A single gravestone was inscribed with the names of two people: Benjamin Winslow and his wife, Phebe. Nothing on the stone indicated that there was a heart buried in the plot. Edward and Dr. Gardner were stumped, so they spoke to several more people to try to piece things together. But after chatting with the cemetery caretaker and the local undertaker, the men came up empty handed.

The two made one last stop at the Nantucket Genealogical Society in hopes that it might have some information on the story. Mrs. Addison T. Winslow from the society promised the two men that she would do some research for them, and later that afternoon, she met with them to reveal what she had found. Mrs. Winslow found a mention of the doctor in papers that were dated 1895, and according to the papers, he had died sometime in 1877 in Salt Lake City. Within just a few hours, Edward was sitting in front of writers from all of the local newspapers, and he was able to unravel the uncanny story.

Dr. Charles F. Winslow was born on June 30, 1811, and according to sources, it was evident very early on that he was an extremely bright young man. He studied at Harvard University and later in Paris, and he became a doctor and a lawyer. In addition, he had a very acute interest in astronomy, and he published a book in 1853 about his theories on atomic reactions in the universe. Dr. Winslow traveled all over the world for the U.S. State Department, and everywhere he went, he amazed people with his knowledge of the universe and the world in general.

When Dr. Winslow's wife died in 1874, he moved to Salt Lake City and practiced law there. It wasn't long after he moved that he wrote his will, which contained very unusual yet specific instructions on what should be done with his body after his death. In the will, Dr. Winslow insisted that forty hours after his death, an anatomist was to remove his heart and place it in a "strong glass vessel [that had] a ground glass stopper accurately fitted." The vessel was to be filled with a mixture of ammonia and embalming fluids to preserve his heart. Once the vessel was sealed, it was to be covered in wet parchment paper and placed inside a thick oak plank box that was to be covered in coal tar and placed in a plain pine case. The box was to be buried over the grave of his mother on the island of Nantucket, where he was born. After he died, these instructions were carried out as he desired. The rest of his body was cremated, and the ashes were sent to Mount Auburn Cemetery in Cambridge, Massachusetts, where they were buried with his wife.

Despite all the information that Edward had found out about Dr. Winslow, there were many on Nantucket who believed that the heart never made it to the island. He, nevertheless, would not give up and went back to see the caretaker. The caretaker eventually agreed to check the grave for the wooden box by poking several long steel rods into the ground. Within moments, Edward and the caretaker discovered that there was a small box that was approximately eighteen inches long and one foot wide. Edward got permission from the late doctor's relatives to have the grave dug up, and the box was exhumed. The box was opened, and indeed, inside was Dr. Winslow's heart inside a jar. A photograph was taken as proof of the unusual burial.

Edward helped raise funds to have a memorial marker placed on the grave site. The white marble stone reads:

The Heart Of
Charles F. Winslow
Lies Buried Here

Edward managed to track down Dr. Winslow's great-granddaughter in Dallas, Texas, and he sent her an invitation to come to Nantucket for the dedication of the grave marker. On Monday, July 14, 1947, Edward and friends and relatives of the Winslow family attended the short service and dedication. Dr. Winslow wanted to be with his wife at Mount Auburn but also with his mother in the place where he had grown up. He achieved both. The cemetery where Winslow's heart is buried is now called Newtown Cemetery.

Abel's Hill Cemetery (Chilmark Cemetery), Chilmark, Martha's Vineyard

Movie stars and common folk still pay their respects at John Belushi's grave in Chilmark.

Shifting sands and thick shrubs of the island landscape on Martha's Vineyard make up the terrain of a quiet cemetery along South Road in the town of Chilmark. Originally known as Abel's Hill Cemetery, it was named for a Native American who was known as Abel who lived in a wigwam at the top of the hill. Many of the oldest gravestones date back to 1717, and protective lead covers have been placed over some of the gravestones to help preserve them. There are said to be a number of Native American graves with simple fieldstone markers in the oldest section of the cemetery. One of the surprising things about the cemetery is all the rare lady-slipper flowers that grow within the grounds. An endangered wild orchid, lady-slippers can go several years without blooming, making their discovery quite special.

A large gravestone with a skull and crossbones near the entrance of the cemetery marks the area where famous Hollywood actor and comedian John Belushi is buried. On March 5, 1982, at the age of thirty-three, John died from respiratory failure brought on from an overdose of drugs. His memorial service in New York drew over one thousand people, including other Hollywood stars. Belushi and his wife had purchased a house not far from the cemetery in Chilmark, and that is why he is buried there. His remains were moved once after he was buried in the cemetery, as there was a bit of vandalism done to his grave, so today, the identifying marker is not directly over his remains. To this day, many celebrities visit the grave site for John Belushi and leave tokens of remembrance, from cigarettes to empty beer cans. Should you visit the grave site and see a famous visitor paying his or her respects, remember Vineyard etiquette and do not take photos or ask for an autograph.

THE CHICKEN WOMAN, NANCY LUCE, WEST TISBURY

The legacy of the "Chicken Woman" of Martha's Vineyard is one filled with laughter and tears. Nancy Luce grew up in the farming village of West Tisbury on Martha's Vineyard. She had a love for horses and riding the country trails. The fondness that she had for farm animals extended to her hens, and as she got older, she found a peace and friendship with them that many people didn't seem to understand. Summer visitors would often make pilgrimages to see her and her unusual ways. Nancy named her chickens unique names such as Teppetee Tappao, Pondy Lily and Beauty Linna. She would often write poetry about her love for the chickens, and she soon became quite a sensation in the press. It was written in the *Atlantic Monthly*:

Nancy Luce, "the chicken lady," was one of the most interesting residents of West Tisbury on Martha's Vineyard.

An old tester bedstead and a massive mahogany bureau seem to glower at us from behind her; a heavily beamed and smoke darkened ceiling frowns from overhead; and a broad, paneled chimney piece forms the prospect upon which her gaze is rather bent upon us. Whenever her glance does turn upon us we meet it with a thrill—a thrill at first of repulsion, then of eeriness, and next pity half blots out both sensations, but not wholly, for she is a grotesque figure.

Despite some of the unfriendly press, visitors flocked like chickens to her home. Nancy wrote in her journal about visitors:

Good behavior of foreign folks
From camp meeting,
They behaved well
And bought books of me.
I cannot live without them.

I want to see tender hearted folks.
I am cast down to the dust of the earth,
With troubles, trials, sickness,
And for sin in the world.

Nancy sold her own photographs of her hens to summer visitors, along with pamphlets of her poems. There seemed to be a lot of pranks that were also pulled by people who stopped in to see her. There are several accounts in the old police logs of incidents with Nancy:

Oct. 26, 1882: Miss Nancy Luce, a maiden lady who lives alone, was visited recently by two unknown young men, and she thought it best to defend herself by showing a pistol. They wrested it from her hands her cries aroused a neighbor, who went to her assistance. She now has a new pistol and claims she has a right to defend herself. During the last day of the Agricultural Fair, twenty carriage loads of people visited her. Some of them carried their fun a little too far by shutting their hostess in a closet, but they made up with her by purchasing a large number of her books.

When Nancy's hens died, she commissioned white marble gravestones for them and wrote poems about how she felt:

O my Poor deceased little Ada Queetie,
She knew such a sight and her love and mine,

Dead on the Tide

A visit to the Martha's Vineyard Museum in Edgartown offers close-up views of a nineteenth-century hearse and the original gravestones for Nancy Luce's chickens.

So deep in our hearts for each other,
The part of her and her undergoing sickness and death,
O heart rending!

One of the most heartfelt things Nancy related in her poems:

Be good and kind to all that breathes,
Act up on our good savour's laws,
Have tender feelings in your hearts
For all the poor harmless dumb creatures.

Nancy died on April 9, 1890, and her house and farm passed into different hands. The gravestones she commissioned for her chickens became doorsteps. Nancy was buried in the West Tisbury Village Cemetery. The memory of her was nearly forgotten until the Martha's Vineyard Museum was able to obtain the gravestones for Nancy's chickens; the museum now has them on display. Nancy's grave in West Tisbury can be found as well-wishers leave chicken mementos and statues by her headstone. Visitors to the cemetery describe being able to find her grave by following the sounds of roosters and chickens, and when the sounds mysteriously stop, they are standing in front of Lucy's grave.

Chapter Four

Gardens of Stone

FOREST HILLS CEMETERY, JAMAICA PLAIN

One of the most beautiful and remarkable nineteenth-century cemeteries in the country, Forest Hills Cemetery in Jamaica Plain offers the visitor a wealth of exquisite Victorian-era memorials. This burial ground is also an arboretum, providing plenty of shade and serving as a sanctuary for birds and urban wildlife.

Forest Hill was commissioned and designed by General Henry A.S. Dearborn, a state senator and congressman. He came up with the design to mark out

> *the winding avenues and shaded paths, observing how each should reveal some beauty while making available the gentle slopes or the rugged steeps as resting places for the dead…He modeled the imposing gateway at the principal entrance; he projected the chief adornments, and in a word, he stamped his own idea upon the cemetery in all the varied forms with which art has developed and increased the beauties of nature, an untiring industry, and a pious regard for the claims of the dead. Hardly was there a sign that he even desired to associate his name so intimately with the sacred shades of Forest Hills…though such an ambition were no unworthy one. But he labored rather for the love of his work, for the honor of the dead and the solace of the living.*

It was believed that in the Victorian era, "nature offered special keys for unlocking the mysteries of life and death." Once, this property was two large sprawling farms, and today, the 250 acres are a final resting place for a

Above: A red-tailed hawk cools off in a birdbath at Forest Hills Cemetery.

Right: The Boy in the Boat grave marker is one of the most detailed sculptures in Forest Hills Cemetery.

An incredible Victorian Gothic mausoleum at Forest Hills Cemetery in Jamaica Plain.

variety of people, even some famous persons such as poets Anne Sexton and E.E. Cummings, playwright Eugene O'Neill and abolitionist William Lloyd Garrison. Forest Hills' landscape is a museum of sculpture, art and monuments that chronicles the Victorian age to the present. The first crematorium in New England was established here in 1893.

One of the most famous monuments at Forest Hills is the Boy in the Boat memorial located on Citron Path. In 1886, while in a small boat near the shore of a pond, five-year-old Louis Mieusset noticed his pet rabbit running along the bank. Little Louis wanted to bring his pet with him in the boat. He reached out for his pet but lost his balance, fell out of the boat and drowned. The monument, commissioned by the boy's mother, Louise Hellium Mieusset, captures the boy's tragic last moment. The marble monument was encased in glass and bronze to preserve it. There are some who come and pay their respects at the grave, as evidenced by the fresh flowers that have been placed at the grave site. No one, however, has been seen keeping a silent vigil.

A walk along Lobelia Path reveals the beautifully preserved white marble statue for little Gracie Allen. The sculpture is encased in glass and has been protected for nearly one hundred years. Carved by Sydney Morse, the lifelike sculpture depicts a young girl in a buttoned dress with boots and bow-tied hair holding drooping flowers, the petals of which have begun to fall (which symbolizes death). Gracie Allen died from whooping cough in 1880, just before her fifth birthday.

The sculpture of a well-dressed man memorializes John Reece, who died in 1896. Reece was an industrialist who invented and patented a buttonhole sewing machine. He died while trying to save an employee in his factory who was in danger of being crushed by a moving elevator. Reece jumped for the elevator rope but missed the cord and fell to his death.

Large Gothic mausoleums are tucked between the hills and perennial flower bushes, and they seem to have become part of the natural landscape over the years. Majestic trees stand guard on the corners of pathways and on sloping hillsides. Due to its picturesque, garden atmosphere, the cemetery was often frequented by sightseers who were taking carriage rides along the pond and shady roads in the nineteenth century.

The nonprofit Forest Hills Educational Trust oversees the cemetery and strives to keep the history and legacy alive by organizing public exhibitions of contemporary art, concerts and poetry readings, walking tours, the Buddhist-inspired Lantern Festival and a traditional Mexican Day of the Dead festival. Maps for further exploration of the cemetery are available at the information area by the massive gatehouse entrance.

The lifelike sculpture of little Grace Allen is one of the most visited grave sites in Forest Hills.

Mount Auburn Cemetery, Cambridge

If there be any wisdom to be gathered among the tombs, useful though hard lessons to be learned…A tomb is, it has been said, a monument on the limits of both worlds; it is a tower on the narrow isthmus that separates life from death, and time from eternity; and standing upon it we look back double regret on the misprized [sic] *and misspent past and our failing resolutions for the dark and boundless future. Shadows, clouds and darkness rest upon it* [and it] *is natural to strive after more perfection and to feel the hopes of hereafter when surrounded by the graves of men who have gone before.*
—New England Magazine *on the dedication of Mount Auburn Cemetery, 1831*

Mount Auburn Cemetery remains one of the most visited cemeteries in the world.

Before the establishment of Mount Auburn Cemetery, people's beliefs about death were dark and gloomy; the grim reaper was everywhere. People were also aware that the cemeteries of Boston were becoming dangerously overfilled, and as aforementioned, bones and coffins regularly became exposed, increasing the risk of widespread disease. General Henry Dearborn, president of the Massachusetts Horticultural Society, felt that the dead should be buried and honored in a place of natural beauty that would lend dignity to death. He felt that the living who were visiting their deceased loved ones needed a welcoming place of beauty that had fountains, ponds, beautiful monuments and ornamental plantings. Using the famous Pere LaChaise Cemetery as a model, Dearborn created the first public landscape in the United States. The grounds at Mount Auburn were consecrated on September 24, 1831, and the garden-style cemetery was born. Later public parks were modeled after this burial ground.

There were more than two thousand people in attendance at the consecration ceremony. Joseph Story, associate justice of the U.S. Supreme Court, spoke at the ceremony. Following is an excerpt:

> *A rural Cemetery seems to combine in itself all the advantages, which can be proposed to gratify human feelings, or tranquilize human fears. And what spot can be more appropriate than this, for such a purpose? Nature seems to point it out…as the favorite retirement for the dead. There are around us all the varied features of her beauty and grandeur—the forest-crowned height, the grassy glade; and the silent grove. Here are the lofty oak, the beech…the rustling pine, and the drooping willow—the tree, that sheds its pale leaves with every autumn, a fit emblem of our own transitory bloom; and the evergreen, with its perennial shoots, instructing us, that "the wintry blast of death kills not the buds of virtue."*

The gravestone for Peter Byus depicts a slave being freed, with broken chains at his feet.

Ascend but a few steps, and what a change of scenery to surprise and delight us. We seem, as it were in an instant, to pass from the confines of death, to the bright and balmy regions of life. Below us flows the winding Charles (River) with its rippling current, like the stream of time hastening to the ocean of eternity. In the distance, the City—at once the object of our admiration and our love—rears...its lofty towers, its graceful mansions, its curling smoke, its crowded haunts of business and pleasure.

We stand, as it were, upon the borders of two worlds; and we may gather lessons of profound wisdom by contrasting the one with the other, or indulge in the dreams of hope and ambition, or solace our hearts by melancholy meditations.

The voice of consolation will spring up in the midst of the silences of these regions of death. The hand of friendship will delight to cherish the flowers, and the shrubs, that fringe the lowly grave, or the sculptured monument... Spring will invite thither the footsteps of the young by its opening foliage; and autumn detain the contemplative. Here let us erect the memorials of our love, and our gratitude, and our glory.

Visitors came from all over, as they still do today, to revel in the cemetery's natural beauty and tranquility. Guidebooks that described the architecture, the artwork and the names of various paintings were offered to the public.

There is a statue of a praying child on the grave of Leopold Morse.

The cemetery features several scenic ponds, and the rolling hills are covered in gravestones and memorial monuments. In fact, in the nineteenth century, many relatives of the deceased who were buried at Mount Auburn hung framed sketches of the burial plots in their homes, which was a dramatic departure from the mourning customs of the eighteenth century. The design and style of the cemetery also illustrate the shift in attitude toward death during that time. Death was no longer something to live in fear of.

The entrance is framed by an Egyptian Revival gateway, which is symbolic of the sacred doorway to the world of the dead. It was rebuilt in 1842 of Quincy granite. The 175-acre cemetery has over five thousand trees, and there are several greenhouses on-site that produce many of the flowers that decorate the grounds. With lanes that have names like Jonquil Path, Azalea Path and Poppy Path, one can't help envision this place as a heavenly garden. The many sculptures that dot the grounds remind one of a fine arts museum.

Some people go to the cemetery to visit the stone dogs, which represent faithfulness and devotion. The Harnden Dog is an English mastiff and keeps watch at the grave of William Frederick Harnden, who died in 1845. The Milmore Dog is somewhat hard to find on the extensive grounds. This monument of a marble whippet sits near the Wingate family plot and is encased in glass. The inscription at the bottom of the monument reads, "Their favorite." A stone Newfoundland dog can be found on the Thomas Perkins plot and is carved out of Italian marble. It was commissioned by Perkins in 1844, six years before his death.

An English setter known as the Gray Dog is curled at the top of the headstone for Francis Calley Gray. Gray was a lawyer, and he served as a private secretary to President John Quincy Adams. The dog was commissioned by Gray's friend, Massachusetts congressman William Appleton. It was originally designed to be on William's grave, but he had it placed on the grave of his friend Francis. Then there is the Saunders Dog, which marks the grave of a child named Mary Prentiss Saunders, who died in 1849 at the age of six. The Richardson Dog is on the grave of Civil War soldier William T. Richardson, who died in 1864 at the age of eighteen. An Irish setter plaintively looks up from a grave marker that bears the name Barnard.

It is difficult to see the entire cemetery in one day, as there is so much to observe and appreciate. The Bigelow Chapel was built in a Gothic Revival style, and Dr. Jacob Bigelow, one of Mount Auburn's founders, wrote that the Gothic style imitated the groves and bowers under which ancient druids performed their sacred rites. The enormous stained-glass windows in the chapel were imported from Edinburgh, Scotland. In front of the stunning Bigelow Chapel sits a massive sphinx, one of the grandest monuments in the cemetery. The statue is fifteen feet high and is a memorial to those who fell in the Civil War. The sphinx is a lion with a human head and is adorned with a pharaoh's headdress and a necklace with a star. The inscriptions on both sides read:

American Union Preserved
African Slavery Destroyed
By the Uprising of a Great People
by the Blood of Fallen Heroes.

The inscription on one of the sides is written in Latin. Dr. Jacob Bigelow also commissioned the massive monument. Prior to its completion, Dr. Bigelow went blind, and he requested to feel every feature of the sphinx before it was set.

Cedar Avenue offers a variety of funerary images carved on the gravestones, including a winged hourglass, a butterfly emerging from a cocoon, broken flowers, ivy and oak and laurel wreaths. One of the most amazing features about the cemetery is the fantastic observation tower that offers a panoramic view of Boston and the surrounding towns. The tower bears the name of whom it was built to honor—George Washington. And the view from it is not to be missed!

Mount Auburn is an internationally known landscape that sees hundreds of thousands of visitors from around the world every year and is the final resting place for many famous people, including Henry Wadsworth Longfellow, Winslow Homer, Oliver Wendell Holmes and Charles Bulfinch. Cemeteries around the country have followed Mount Auburn's lead and emulated its peaceful and welcoming design for burial of the dead.

LOWELL CEMETERY

Located on the south side of Lowell is the scenic Lowell Cemetery, which was dedicated in June 1841. Taking its design from Mount Auburn, the cemetery emphasized the physical beauty of the surroundings and created a comforting sanctuary to visitors. There are fascinating mausoleums situated behind a variety of beautiful, shady trees. A variety of blooming rosebushes highlights the hillsides and walkways. There are many memorials throughout the cemetery that make the location legendary.

One of the most beautiful monuments is the magnificent Ayer lion. The face of the lion is rather sorrowful, and the detail is quite extraordinary for being carved out of stone. Measuring eight feet high with a thirteen-foot base, the piece weighs about twenty-five tons. A memorial fund established by the Ayer estate provides care for the lion in the winter months, when it is covered with a protective wooden encasement.

A short walk from the Ayer lion is the often-visited Clara Bonney memorial. The dramatic memorial is the subject of many local legends and lore. There is usually a collection surrounding the monument of flowers, beads and coins left by well-wishers. The visits to the Bonney memorial increase as it gets closer to Halloween, and offerings pile up on the ground. The popular rumor that Clara was a convicted witch is untrue, as she passed away in 1894 and not in the late seventeenth century during the witchcraft hysteria. Despite the facts, curious folks continue to visit the memorial, perpetuating the story. Clara was the wife of Charles Sumner Lilly and a local millworker; there is no existing documented information about her being associated with witchcraft.

While the monument is striking, there are misunderstandings about the meaning of the design. The woman depicted is an image that can be seen in various interpretations around the cemetery and is called "beyond the veil." The veil represents the curtain between the world of the living and the world of the dead; in some interpretations, it is what lies beyond this life. The woman in the sculpture holds the veil over her head, offering a glimpse into the spirit world. This type of imagery became popular in Victorian times, especially during the Spiritualist movement, and is reflected on many monuments and memorials in Lowell Cemetery.

Gardens of Stone

Above: The Ayer lion is one of the most unusual monuments in Lowell Cemetery.

Right: Truly an urban legend, the stories about "witch" Clara Bonney are based largely on the striking design of her memorial.

Chapter Five

Silent Stones and the Voices of the Dead

FOREFATHERS BURYING GROUND, CHELMSFORD

One of the oldest cemeteries in Merrimack Valley, the Forefathers Burying Ground is located along Route 110 in Chelmsford. The burial ground was established in 1655, and the oldest remaining dated stone is from 1690. There are also a number of field stone markers that indicate older graves. The oldest section of the grounds is easy to find as all of the gravestones face east. It was believed during the seventeenth and eighteenth centuries that the buried should face eastward so that when Judgment Day arrived, they could rise up out of the grave, face their Holy Creator and be judged according to the deeds of their lives.

Among the many interesting gravestones and epitaphs found within the cemetery is that of Elizabeth Clark. The gravestone depicts a trumpeting angel clearing a path through growing leaves and vines. Two round cherub faces can be found on the borders, and there is a scallop shell in the center. The inscription reads:

Here lies Interr'd the Remains of Mrs Elizabeth Clark the Wife of Jonas Clark Esqr Who departed this Life April 27ᵗʰ 1767. Ag'd 74 Years.

Halt passenger as you go past,
Remember time, it runeth fast,
My dust in narrow pounds do ly,
Remember man that thou must dye,
This dust revive it shall again,
And in a grave no more remain,

When Trumpet sounds I shall be rais'd,
For thus God's Holy word hath said.

The gravestone for Jonas Clark depicts two large, flying angels. One of them is carrying a Bible, and the other is holding a trumpet. A portrait of a colonial-style man is engraved in the stone's center. There are also two vases with flowers, fleur-de-lis and scallop shells on the borders. Jonas was the son of Reverend Thomas Clark. Reverend Clark hoped that his son would follow in his footsteps and become a preacher himself. Jonas, however, decided to pursue business instead. He built a tavern in Middlesex Village (known today as Lowell), and the tavern eventually came to be known as Clark's Tavern. Jonas also owned a ferry that crossed the Merrimack River, which helped make him the wealthiest man in the community.

Here lies interr'd the Body of Coln [sic] Jonas Clark
who departed this Life April 28th 1770
In the 86th year of his age.

God's creatures are his own, their lives
He may at pleasure take, when he resumes but what he gives,
who can objections make?

Thessaolonians IV 16. For the Lord himself shall defeend [sic]
from heaven with ashout,
with the voice of the arch angel,
and the trump of God & the dead in Christ shall rise first.

John Stickelmire was a German immigrant who worked as a glass blower at the Chelmsford Glass Works. The poem and inscription on his grave describe his occupation.

sacred
To the memory of
John J. Stickelmire,
a Nativ & of GERMANY, and late foreman of
the Chelmsford Glass Manufactory,
Died March 31st 1814
Aged 48 years.

This verse reminds the heedless as they pass
That life's a fragile drop of unnealed glass,

The slightest wound ensures a fatal burst
And the frail fabric shivers into dust.
So he whom in his art could none surpass,
Is now himself reduced to broken glass,
But from the grave, the fining pot of man,
From scandiver and galss [sic] galls purged again,
New mixed and fashioned by almighty power,
Shall rise a firmer fabric than before.

One of the most dramatic gravestones is for Oliver Fletcher, who was the town clerk of Chelmsford in the eighteenth century. The stone displays a 3D lifelike skull with a partial vertebrae. Because the skull is so large, there is barely any room for the inscription, which reads:

Memento Mori
Oliver Fletcher Esq.
Departed this life Nov. 30, 1771
In the 63ᵈ Year of his age
And his remains are here interred

Another stone not to be missed in the burying ground is the large one for Mrs. Hannah Fletcher. Carved on the stone are five heads, one for Mrs. Fletcher who died on September 26, 1778, and one for each of her children, who died under the age of ten. The smallpox epidemic took all five family members, as well as other members of the town. Because there was no modern medicine and no vaccinations, the communities where disease raged could do nothing except try to survive these outbreaks. The children, who had weaker immune systems, were always hit the hardest.

The gravestone for young Job Spaulding is a reminder of how young some of the men who served in the Revolutionary War were.

Job Spaulding
Born March 1762
Died November 15, 1835

A Revolutionary Pensioner, Honorably discharged, from
The first three years service of his Country
May 1780, at the early age of 18 yrs. & 2 mos.
An honest man.

The Arsenic Stone, Pelham

One of Massachusetts's most legendary gravestones can be found in the town of Pelham at Knights Cemetery located on Packardville Road. The stone reads:

Warren Gibbs
Died by arsenic poison
Mar. 23, 1860
AE 36 years 5 mos. 23 days

Think my friends when this you see
How my wife hath dealt by me
She in some oysters did prepare
Some poison for my lot and share;
When of the same I did partake
And nature yielded to its fate
Before she my wife became
Mary Felton was her name.

Warren had become quite ill during the late winter of 1860, and concerned townsfolk stopped by his house to bring him cider in hopes that he would recover. Warren's wife, Mary, prepared him a plate of oysters, and after consuming it, he died within a few days. Warren's brother William was so certain that his death was no accident that he commissioned the telling stone. Mary's family was upset by the accusation and had the stone removed. William replaced the stone and allegedly put a curse on anyone who attempted to remove it. The stone was vandalized over the years, and the Pelham Historical Society has what is believed to be the original stone. A replacement has been placed on the grave in case it is stolen again.

There are some who debate where the stone ended up because a man named Professor Valentine who worked at Springfield College bought a farm in town in the 1940s, and on the grounds, he unearthed the same exact gravestone for Warren Gibbs. He turned the stone over to authorities, but no one is sure which one is the original gravestone. Whatever the case may be, the current stone that stands on Warren's grave is a replacement, but it still attracts the attention of local curiosity seekers.

WESTERN BURIAL GROUND, LYNN

The city of Lynn, Massachusetts, was established in 1629, and one of its oldest cemeteries is the Western Burying Ground (also known as the Old Burying Ground), which dates back to 1637. This simple cemetery is located in an urban residential neighborhood and was used up until the late nineteenth century. It is believed that many who were buried here later were not buried six feet deep. In the 1840s, the cemetery suffered from overcrowding; bones pushed through the surface on a fairly regular basis. The cemetery caretaker actually paid the neighborhood children to clean up the cemetery. They were paid by the bone, so the more bones they turned in, the more money they made.

One of the most famous people buried in the cemetery is Mary "Moll" Pitcher, the famous fortuneteller. Her father was the well-known wizard Old Dimond of Marblehead. She has a fairly simple white marble gravestone that bears her name and her birth and death years (1738–1813). Her legacy and story is one that is still discussed today by the locals.

There are many broken stones in the cemetery, and there are a lot of eighteenth-century slate markers, many of which have fascinating epitaphs. Here is one example:

The hand of affection hath raised this stone to tell the passing traveller that here lies buried the body of Mary Ann, wife of Aaron Bacheller who died June 6, 1824, AEt. 19 years and ten months.

Her days were few & quickly told,
Her life, a mournful story,
Hath ended like the morning star,
That melts in deeper glory.

The beautifully preserved gravestone of Dr. John Henry Burchstead features angels, spirals and swirls. Burchstead himself was from the Slavic area of Europe called Silesia, which once comprised Germany, Poland and the Czech Republic.

Here lyes buried ye body of Doc'r JOHN—HENRY Burchsted, a Silesian; who died Sept'br XX, Anno Christi, MDCCXXI, AEtatis Suae LXIII [63 years].
Silesia to New England sent this man,
To do their all that any healer can,
But he who conquered all diseases must

Find one who throws him down into the dust.
A. chymist near to an adeptit come,
Leaves here, thrown by, his caput mortuum.
Reader, physicians die as others do;
Prepare, for thou to this art hastening too.

A very simple marble stone tells the fascinating tale of a soldier:

Died at Gettysburg July 4, 1863, John Quincy Burrill, Aged 22 years.
He was a member of the 1ˢᵗ Mass. Reg't and was killed in the battle of
Gettysburg, PA., while gallantly fighting for his country beneath the folds of
her starry flag.
"How sleep the brave who sink to rest,
By all their country's wishes blest."

Harriet Burrill, died April 30, 1851. AEt. 40.
"She taught us how to live, and O, too high
The price of knowledge, taught us how to die."
"Death is the gate to endless joy."

In memory of Mr. John Cheever who died Aug. 12, 1834, AEt. 44.
His course is run, his spirit's fled,
He joins the mansion of the dead;
He now lies cold, but now his soul,
Will live till ages cease to roll.

A large double stone for two children with two willow trees reads:

In memory of two children of Mr. Joseph & Mrs. Hephzibath Cheever.
Anna, died Sept. 16, 1816, AEt. 2 years
Joseph Warren, died Oct. 9, 1821, AEt. 18 months.
Beneath this tomb two infants lie,
Say, are they lost or saved?
If death by sin, they sinned for they lie here;
If heaven by works, they can't in heaven appear.
Revere the sacred page, the knot untied;
They died, for Adam sinned;
They live, for Jesus died.

In Memory of
Amos Ballard, son of
Mr. John Ballard
of Bofton
who was deprived of life
by the accidental discharge
of a musket in a canoe
in Lynn River
on the 25th of Aug. 1798
AEt. 77

Chapter Six

Bone Chilling Tales

A Souvenir of Death, Newburyport

Reverend George Whitefield was born in Gloucester, England, in 1714, and he was said to be a wonderful speaker. He arrived in Newburyport in 1740 but traveled many times back and forth across the Atlantic. His sermons drew so many people that he would often hold them outdoors to accommodate the large crowds that sometimes numbered fifteen thousand. Benjamin Franklin even expressed his fondness and admiration of Reverend Whitefield after hearing one of his sermons.

Whitefield passed away at Jonathan Parsons's Newburyport home thirty years after his first visit to the town. He was so beloved by the people that residents in both Boston and Portsmouth, New Hampshire, wanted him to be buried in their cities, while friends in England wanted his body shipped home. The decision was made to bury him in Newburyport underneath the pulpit in the First Presbyterian Church on Federal Street. The reverend was buried in his minister's gown and wig, and the coffin lid was kept open so that visitors could view his remains. But one visitor did more than just pay his respects to the reverend.

In 1829, during a remodel of the church, the reverend and several other ministers were disinterred, and it was discovered that the reverend's right arm was missing. It was thought that a serious admirer of Whitefield's needed a souvenir to take with him. According to the story, the mystery man paid a friend who, with the help of the sexton's son, took the bones. Once people on both sides of the Atlantic heard about what had happened, they were outraged. Almost twenty years later, the conscience of the souvenir-grabbing thief must have gotten to him because he decided to make amends. The thief contracted a Newburyport captain to see to it that the arm was restored to the minister. The captain delivered the bony package and an apologetic letter to the minister of the church.

The crypt can be visited on tours of Old South Church, along with the bell cast by Paul Revere. Guests can also visit the Whispering Galleries and the slave pews. The arm, however, is tucked safely out of view in the reverend's tomb.

A bronze plaque next to the burial chamber reads:

George Whitefield
1714–1770

I am content to wait till the day
Of judgment for the clearing
Up of my character; and after I am
Dead I desire no other epitaph
Than this, "Here lies G.W. What
Sort of he was the great day
Will discover"

COPP'S HILL BURYING GROUND, BOSTON

Copp's Hill Burying Ground is the second oldest burying ground in Boston, after King's Chapel. This is the largest graveyard in Boston and is located near the famous Old North Church. The grounds were named after William Copp, a former owner of the land, and many of his descendants are buried here. The cemetery is composed of four different sections: the Old North Burying Ground, Hull Street Burying Ground, Charter Street Burying Ground and the New North Burying Ground. Each section was purchased at a separate time as the cemetery continued to expand over the years. It was estimated in 1882 that over ten thousand persons have been buried here. In the nineteenth century, there were 230 tombs, 2 of which belonged to the City of Boston. The tomb near Charter Street was said to have been fitted and prepared for children in June 1833.

The British had once occupied Copp's Hill because of its strategic height and view, and they used it to train their cannons on Charlestown during the Battle of Bunker Hill. The hill is not as high as it used to be, as it has been continually altered by man over the years.

There are numerous stories of graves being desecrated at Copp's Hill. A woman who was a regular visitor to the graveyard said that she saw heaps of

The atrocities suffered by many of the dead who rest in Copp's Hill Burying Ground are documented in Boston's public records.

coffins stacked up and some of the remnants of their former occupants. The coffins had pieces of clothing visible, and they were broken apart in some cases. Skin residue and even long black hair adhered to the caskets. These deeds were supposedly committed by grave diggers seeking to make a fortune in one night by grave robbing. No one was certain where the bodies were taken, but quite a few speculated that they were carted out of the cemetery in the middle of the night and dumped, one on top of another, and crushed into hideous masses to make additional room for more burials.

Tales of disinterment by those who were respected in the community were also fairly commonplace. One such story concerns Samuel Winslow, who was the church sexton in charge of the maintenance of the graveyard. The beautiful coat of arms on one tomb must have been appealing to Samuel, who had the bodies removed so that he could use it as a temporary resting place for those who would soon be buried at Copp's Hill. Samuel was so bold that he removed the name of William Clark from the tomb and had his own inscribed on there.

Another tomb that was altered belonged to the Hutchinson family and was situated near the southeast corner of the cemetery. A square slab of sandstone with a beautiful coat of arms covers its entrance. The name Hutchinson has been cut out and replaced with the name Thomas Lewis, who had no ties to the family. Thomas and Elisha Hutchinson, the father and grandfather of the governor of Massachusetts during the time of the Stamp Act, once rested in a vault beneath this tablet. While details of Thomas's death are unknown, Elisha was killed in an Indian attack in Brookfield. The two were descendants of Ann Hutchinson and her husband, Governor William. No one knows for sure where the final resting places of the Hutchinsons are today.

While there is a large assortment of gravestones from the seventeenth and eighteenth centuries, many have been lost for a variety of reasons. For example, in December 1878, the superintendent of Copp's Hill opened an old tomb and discovered a headstone from 1713. The tomb had not been opened for eighteen years, and the last undertaker to close it blocked the entrance with gravestones before filling it with dirt. Many stones will never see the light of day because they were placed in the bottoms of the tombs for coffins to rest on.

In 1878, twenty-two grave markers that belonged to Copp's Hill were finally recovered. Two were being used as chimney tops, while two others covered drains. Others were found in the cellars of homes in the area. A tombstone was discovered when Commercial Street was being widened at the foot of Lime Alley, four feet below the surface. Its inscription read, "Elizabeth Boone, aged 2 years, Dyed ye 13 October 1677." These stones were randomly placed back in the burial ground, as there was no way to figure out where they truly belonged.

The terrain of the cemetery also presented challenges over the years. Dirt paths had to be concreted over as the rain washed away the soil, creating gullies where the water collected. During heavy rains, so much dirt was washed away that the tops of coffins became visible.

During the nineteenth century, the cemetery was surrounded by tenement houses, and the tenants would string their clotheslines across the burial ground and attach them to the trees that stand inside the cemetery. The graveyard was also overrun with house cats during those years.

There are a handful of stones from the mid-seventeenth century that had their dates altered by vandals, which makes identifying the oldest stone in the burial ground difficult. The dates on the gravestones were altered by carving over the numbers, and the most common change was modifying the number nine into the number two, so that a stone that read 1690 was changed to 1620. This happened in several of Boston's burial grounds.

There are purported to be thousands of free African Americans who lived in an area of Boston called New Guinea buried here as well, and most of them lie in unmarked graves.

There are various interesting stories about the inhabitants of the cemetery. One is about a captain who was killed in Maine during an Indian assault. His body was riddled with bullets, which were removed and melted down. The lead was then poured into an opening on his slate grave marker. The metal has been hewn out over the years by neighborhood kids with knives, leaving the slit filled with gravel and scant traces of lead. The stone can be found in the northwest section of the burial ground. The inscription reads:

capt thomas lake
aged 61 yeeres
an eminently faithfull servant
of god & one of a public spirit
was perfidiously slain by
ye indians at kennibeck
august ye 14th 1676
& here interred the 13 of
march following

There's a story locals tell about a "wishing rock" that sits on the edge of the cemetery near the corner of Charter Street. The children used the flat surface of the rock as a playground, and they would dance in groups and sing around it as a means of sending forth their wishes. One day while the children were singing and circling the rock, the ground underneath them suddenly gave way, and several of them fell into a forgotten underground well. The children were finally rescued by passersby who happened to be in the area.

Some notable people buried at Copp's Hill include Robert Newman, the Old North Church sexton who hung the lanterns on the night of Paul Revere's famous midnight ride; Prince Hall, who is considered the founder of "black Freemasonry"; and fire and brimstone preachers Cotton and Increase Mather. Cotton Mather was a respected Boston minister who wrote about many religious topics. His 1689 book *Memorable Providences* describes a case of supposed witchcraft that had occurred in Boston the previous year. Three children had begun acting strangely after a disagreement with an Irish washwoman named Mary Glover. After examining the children, Mather concluded that they were innocent victims of Glover's witchcraft. His sermons and written works fanned the flames of the witchcraft hysteria in Salem, Massachusetts. He declared that the devil was at work in Salem and that witches should face the harshest punishment.

The epitaphs below impart the sentiments of the times:

Sacred to the Memory of
MRS BETSEY PITMAN
wife to Mr Joseph Pitman

who departed this life March 8ᵗʰ
1784
aged 27 years

Haste! haste! He lies in wait. He watches at the door.
Insidious Death! Should his strong hand arrest,
No composition sets the prisoner free.
Death's terror is the mountain faith removes.
'Tis faith disarms destruction.
Believe, and taste the pleasures of a God!
Believe, and look with triumph on the grave.

In Memory of
CAPT ROBERT NEWMAN
who died March 23ᵈ 1806
Aged 51
Though Neptune's waves & Boreas blasts
Have tost me to and fro
Now well escaped from all their rage
I'm anchored here below
Safely I ride in triumph here
With many of our fleet
Till signals call to weigh again
Our Admiral Christ to meet
O may all those I've left behind
Be washed in Jesus' blood
And when they leave this world of sin
Be ever with the Lord

In Memory of
BETSEY,
Wife of David Darling, died
March 23ᵈ, 1809,
Æ. 43.

She was the mother of 17 children, and around
her lies 12 of them, and two were lost at sea.
BROTHER SEXTONS,

Please to leave a clear berth for me
near by this stone.

David Darling was a grave digger at Copp's Hill when the stone was placed there for his wife, Betsey. He was also sexton of the Old North Church and lived on nearby Salem Street. He died in September 1820. He had requested that he be buried next to his wife as indicated by the message on the stone. But David's request was ignored, and he was buried some distance from his wife and family elsewhere in the cemetery. There is no monument to David's memory anywhere in the graveyard.

The chipped and flaking old tombstones that stand under the trees at Copp's Hill have earned our respect, and they connect us with our nation's past. Many of the buried's stories have been lost to the passage of time, but when we remember them, we breathe life back into this old city of the dead.

Old Hadley Cemetery, Hadley

Old Hadley Cemetery located on Cemetery Road dates back to 1660, and it is the final resting place for one of the most notable witches in the early history of Hampshire County—Mary Webster. Mary and her husband, William, were poor and lived for many years in a small house in a meadow near the town. Mary was said to have had a fiery temper, and she used harsh words when she was offended. Neighbors in the farming community who walked cattle and horses to and from the meadow worried when they went past her door. People believed that she would bewitch their animals. Some would stop abruptly when they approached her house and run the other way. The teamsters who walked the animals would go to Mary's door and threaten to whip her, so she would then let the team pass along the road. Once, a wagon with a load of hay that was being driven by her house was mysteriously overturned, and when the driver went to Mary's door, she made a motion, and the wagon turned upright.

There were so many incidents that involved Mary and her bewitching ways that everyone for miles around believed that she was a witch. She was even said to have used dark magic on an infant and made it levitate three times. In a neighboring house, a hen came down the chimney and was scalded in a pot. Not long after, Mary Webster was found suffering from a burn, and people believed that Mary had shape-shifted into a chicken. A local deacon named Philip Smith claimed that she had cursed him. The deacon was very much respected in the community and was one of the original settlers who had come over from England. Mary Webster appeared before the county court on witchcraft charges in Northampton on March 27, 1683. In April, she was sent to the court in Boston. Governor Bradstreet, Deputy Governor Danforth and a jury of nine acquitted Mary of all charges.

Deacon Smith died at the age of fifty-two on January 10, 1685, and Mary Webster was blamed for his death. Cotton Mather comments on the deacon's death in his book *Magnalia* (1702): "Such a man in the winter of the year 1684 was murdered by hideous witchcraft that filled all parts of New England with astonishment. He was by his office concerned about the misery of a wretched woman in the town. He believed he had been receiving wicked mischief at her hands."

The accounts describing the circumstances of Deacon Smith's death only led to more rumors of Mary being a witch. Pots of medicines provided for the sick man were reportedly emptied without explanation, and mysterious scratches were found on the bed. While the deacon's hands and feet were held down by visitors, there seemed to be an invisible source that caused a disturbance. It was even said that flames would appear on the bed and had to be brushed away by those visiting his bedside. People said that they could feel something moving across the bed that they could not see, and this creature was described as being as big as a cat. When Deacon Smith finally died, strange marks were found on his corpse. There was a swelling on one side of his chest, and his back was bruised. There were also several holes that, based on accounts, looked to have been made with awls. Astonishingly, the body remained warm for two days with no signs of life whatsoever. On the third morning, the deacon's face immediately became discolored, turning black and then blue. Chairs in an adjacent room started to shake, and then fresh blood ran down from the top of Smith's head onto his cheeks.

While the deacon was dying, local Hadley boys went to Mary's house, dragged her out and hanged her from a tree until her body became numb with the cold. Her body was cut down and buried in the snow, and she was left for dead. Amazingly, she survived the appalling assault. In fact, she lived for quite a few more years before dying peacefully on June 3, 1698, at the age of eighty-one. Mary was even buried in the same cemetery as Deacon Smith.

A MORBID FASCINATION WITH DEATH—WILMINGTON

The late nineteenth century brought two remarkable people to the town of Wilmington, Massachusetts. The funeral stories of Dr. Hiller and his wife, Frances, are so amazing and unusual that it makes one wonder what lies beneath their simple gravestones in Wildwood Cemetery. Henry Hiller was a doctor from Mannheim, Germany, and he met Frances when he went to London, England. The two were married in 1868 and decided to finally settle in a suburb of Boston where Hiller could serve a large population with his medical practice. The couple built a fourteen-room house, which was quite a spectacle in the town as no one had ever seen anything like it. The house was outfitted with several large, ornate stained-glass windows, imported European wallpaper and an oversized mahogany staircase complete with a carved five-foot alligator with an open mouth.

Dr. Hiller had his office in Boston on Tremont Street, and he quickly become famous for the special elixir he produced there. The medicine he patented was rumored to cure "anything that ailed man or beast." According to the medical journals of the day, his elixir was especially prized for being a "revitalizer of youth and energy." Besides being a delicious concoction of roots and herbs, the elixir had a high alcohol content, which may have been one reason why it was so popular. The medicine proved to be quite popular and, as a result, quite profitable, bringing in about $4,000 a week.

The doctor and his wife, while affluent and eccentric, were quite generous with people in the community of Wilmington. Dr. Hiller would pay for home repairs for those who could not afford them. In some instances, the doctor would buy the house from the person who had financial troubles, completely repair it and then just give it back to them for free. Mrs. Hiller would hold tea for the ladies in town and then take them over to the millinery in Woburn, where she would buy each of them an expensive hat.

Mrs. Hiller would often be seen gardening in full Victorian dress, with black gloves and diamond rings on every finger (including her thumbs), her elbows deep in soil. She had quite a regal appearance. She often carried an ornate parasol and dressed in the finest imported silks and satins. Every night, Mr. and Mrs. Hiller would take a stroll, arm in arm, down the main street in town.

For all their prosperity and happiness, the couple did face many tragedies in their marriage. Mrs. Hiller gave birth to twenty-three children—including seven sets of twins—all of whom died in infancy. The sadness of their losses stayed with them, although Mrs. Hiller believed that it happened because of God's will.

The Hillers were quite interested in the Spiritualist movement, which was quite popular in America during the nineteenth century. The couple regularly spoke about the hereafter and other matters of a spiritual nature with people who were interested. The Hillers decided to think about their funerals and how they wanted them furnished. Dr. Hiller made a contract for coffins with the famous Scottish woodcarver from Cambridge, James MacGreggor. The carvings on the coffins would take seven years to complete and would require a forty-dollar payment each week until they were done. The first coffin to be constructed was to be Mrs. Hiller's; the doctor, however, would be the one to die first. On November 7, 1888, the doctor, at the age of forty-three, died from injuries he had sustained after being thrown from his carriage. His coffin was not ready, so his body was placed in a temporary vault in Winchester for the next year. On September 1, 1889, MacGreggor completed the coffin, and the doctor's funeral was set for September 4, 1889. Following is an account of Dr. Hiller's funeral that was published in an 1890 New York journal:

The doctor's funeral took place just a year ago and the corpse was carried to its last resting place in a silk lined[,] gold plated[,] elaborately carved casket of solid mahogany inclosed [sic] *by another casket no less extravagantly appointed. Six richly caparisoned* [sic] *coal black Percherons* [horses] *in gold mounted harness each attended by a colored groom carried the casket to the temporary vault. There, the doctor's body has been guarded night and day by a grim old watchman. A $500 lamp standing in front has shed its bright rays in the path of possible body snatchers or grave desecrators and every morning the faithful widow has gone to see that everything about the place was all right. Not satisfied with the ghostly magnificence of a year ago the widow has been at work on the construction of new caskets[,] one for her husband the other for herself which easily surpass in magnificence and grotesqueness of ornamentation anything of the kind the world has ever seen. Each casket is in two parts[:] the casket proper and the sarcophagus. The material in all four is solid mahogany* [that was] *imported…from South America. The upholstering inside is as elaborate as money could make it. Corded silk of the value of $40 a yard is the material used. The lids are made of separate panels* [that are] *highly polished* [and] *richly carved and fastened by solid gold hinges with knobs of solid gold for opening them. The doctor's new casket is fastened by a heavy brass door of gothic design* [and has] *a knob made of six pounds of solid gold. On the panels are solid gold tablets inscribed with the doctor's favorite passages of scripture such as I know that my Redeemer liveth, Blessed are they that die in the Lord. Standing at the head of the coffin is a figure of the doctor built out of solid mahogany and reduced to a height of eighteen inches. About him are the figures of four angels welcoming him to paradise.*

It was also written in a newspaper in Pittsburgh, Pennsylvania, called the *Pittsburg Leader* that the coffin had a skull carved out of wood that featured a lizard crawling out of its eye socket. There were also carvings (in the four-inch-thick mahogany) of bats flying over serpents and a big owl holding a field mouse in his talons. The brass work on the coffin was proudly displayed in the maker's shop windows on Portland Street in Boston before the interment. The coffin weighed over two thousand pounds and was five feet tall. It cost $30,000.

According to the *Pittsburg Leader*:

> *Mrs Hiller's coffin on the other hand has her figure recumbent on the lid with three angels ministering to her and the doctor kneeling beside her with his right arm supporting her head. But the most remarkable feature of this remarkable burial casket is the carving on one of the side panels. The sculptor has drawn a sketch of landscape showing at intervals a meadow[,] a river[,] a hill[,] a forest[,] a valley and last of all a mountain at the apex of which is a white cross. Clinging to the cross is a naked cherub and behind another and another until twenty three are counted climbing toward the cross…The procession up the mountain she says perpetuates the memory of her little ones. Mrs. Hiller has also made for herself a burial robe of which it may be truly said that it beggars description. The dressmaker completed it after four months labor and an outlay of $20,000. The robe is made of white ottoman silk corded heavily. There is also a wilderness of white silk and lace running in perpendicular panels and tucked and gathered and fluted until it stands out to a distance of five inches. Between the panels of silk and lace are intermediate panels solely of daisies made in France of pure silk. It is estimated that 5,000 of these daisies are sewed into this gown. The robe opens in front and is fastened by upward of two hundred solid silver hooks designed like a serpent's head. The total outlay by Mrs. Hiller will be not far short of $500,000.*
>
> *The mausoleum will be of hammered granite. In the four walls will be built windows through which it is planned to have rays of colored light enter a different light to each window which blending will fall upon the caskets resting side by side within. The caskets will stand each on four huge brass legs and chairs of magnificent design will be in the mausoleum for the accommodation of sight seers. Mrs. Hiller will soon hold a reception for exhibition of her caskets[,] the invitation to which is a picture of a coffin with ["]Admit one["] written beneath. Mrs. Hiller says Queen Victoria sent to her for all the American papers that contained notices of the doctor's funeral. When she had read them she said that Mrs. Hiller was the only woman who had surpassed her majesty in doing honor to a dead consort.*

After Mrs. Hiller received her coffin, she put it on display in her parlor, and she invited her friends to come over and view it. With a crowd gathered around the coffin, she would climb in and lay down so people would be able to see what she looked like. Mrs. Hiller was disappointed that she couldn't view herself in the coffin, so she had a lifesize wax model of herself made, and she dressed it in the $20,000 funeral robe described above. To show off the coffin to an even wider audience, Mrs. Hiller rented space at the Horticultural Hall in Boston, and she put it on display for $1 admission. The show didn't do very well, and she actually lost money on it.

Five years after Dr. Hiller died, Mrs. Hiller sent out shocking invitations to friends and family. The invitations read that at 2:00 p.m. on Easter Sunday, April 2, 1893, the Hillers were going to renew their marriage vows at their home in Wilmington. People were confused as to what was going on with the marriage. Apparently, the Hillers' loyal, twenty-three-year-old coachman, Peter Surrette, had proclaimed his love to Mrs. Hiller and proposed. Peter was a good man, and his intentions with Mrs. Hiller appeared to be honest and true. She had him sign a prenuptial agreement and requested that he legally change his name to Henry Hiller. The two were married, and their union was much talked about among the townspeople. After an extended illness, just seven years after her second marriage, Mrs. Frances Hiller died.

Thousands of people came from miles around to see what was deemed the funeral of the century. Reporters and crowds packed the town of Wilmington hoping to get a closer look at the coffin as it went along the procession. It took ten men to move the coffin, and it had to be taken out of a side window of the Hiller house. The men rested the coffin on the veranda railing of the house for a moment, and the railing broke. Several men from the crowd had to assist to keep it from crashing to the ground. When the coffin was placed in the funeral car, the weight of it tilted the entire carriage and almost overturned it completely. Four black horses that were draped in black pulled the car, but the car was too high to go under the trolley wires, so the wires had to be cut down by fourteen inches so the car could make its way through.

The procession went down Middlesex Avenue to St. Thomas Church, and onlookers had to be pushed back by police so the casket could be brought in. After the services, Mrs. Hiller was laid to rest in the mausoleum at Wildwood Cemetery. The spectacle and enthralled crowds were just what Mrs. Hiller wanted. Sadly, in 1935, the town decided to take down the Hiller mausoleum, as it had become an "eyesore." The ground was leveled, the mausoleum was destroyed and the well-preserved coffins were removed. All that is visible in memory of Dr. and Mrs. Hiller are two large granite planters and brass nameplates.

THE GRAVE OF THE MAD SCIENTIST, MALDEN

The quiet town of Malden, Massachusetts, is located just north of Boston. The town was originally settled in 1640 and was once a part of Charlestown. In 1649, the town was incorporated. The majority of the settlement was built on scenic hills. The early inhabitants of Malden either engaged in farming or fishing, and with the Mystic River nearby, the community grew quickly. Some men became woodsmen and cleared the dense woods that once existed in Malden. However, almost two hundred years after Malden was settled, one of its residents chose a darker course of work. It was the mid-1800s, and Ephraim Gray lived in an old house in the center of town. That distinctive house was just as worn and wrinkled as its reclusive owner.

Ephraim wasn't married, and he had no relatives or friends; his only companion was a male servant who tended to his needs. Moody and some say misunderstood, Ephraim preferred lurking around his house during the nighttime hours, engaging in strange studies. It was said that odors of repulsive chemicals crept from his house, and people passing by at night would choke and gasp at the horrid smell. Those who chose to look up into the windows of the ominous house saw looming shadows that many described as goblin-like in nature, and many people were afraid just to walk down that side of the street.

Finally, in the year 1850, Ephraim was on his deathbed. He called to his servant and whispered with his last breath, "In my life, I have differed from other men, and by the foul fiend I will continue different after I am dead. My flesh is not common flesh, like yours. It will never rot." When his master passed, Ephraim's servant went to the police station and reported his employer's death. The servant stood to inherit Ephraim's entire estate; however, he did need to see that his master's final wishes were carried out. Ephraim's final request was that his body be left undisturbed from the time of his death until his interment in the local burial ground. That meant no autopsy, no embalming, no removal of fluids or any disturbance to the flesh in any way. The local mortician was horrified at the request; he couldn't understand why Ephraim wouldn't want the usual procedure done to preserve his body. Ephraim's servant explained the strange reasoning behind the request. Ephraim was an accomplished chemist, and he had dedicated most of his later years to devising a formula and method for a youthful elixir that could create immortality. Despite the endless research and formulas, Ephraim's dream of eternal life was never fully realized. However, he made sure to ingest a potion every day that he strongly believed would keep his corpse fresh after death. Ephraim's wishes were honored, and his body was finally entombed five feet deep in the cold ground. The large tomb had an ornate iron door with a decorative granite gable, and those few souls who peered in between the railings of the door were now more curious than ever.

It was about twenty years after Ephraim Gray's death that some curious medical students from Harvard University began discussing the story of the mad scientist from Malden. They were interested in finding out if Ephraim's body still showed signs of life. So one night, the students climbed aboard a carriage in the late hours of the night and took the ride from Cambridge to Malden. It was just after midnight as the carriage rode up to the old burial ground. The students cautiously looked around to make sure that they would not be seen. They went up to the gate, and after much effort, the group was able to push open the heavy iron door. They stepped on to the damp, mossy floor and walked over to the coffin. With a chisel, they pried the lid off the moldering coffin. The lid was pushed back, and a cloud of dirt and dust puffed through the air. The students stared in shock at Ephraim Gray's body. While the clothing on his body was decaying, the body looked much like it had in life, except it had grown brown, hard and dreadful looking. Perhaps Ephraim's body preserving elixir had worked to some extent. The students replaced the coffin lid and snuck back out of the tomb into the moonlit burial ground. After seeing the body for themselves, the students decided that they would try to find out the formula for the preserving elixir. Weeks passed, and the students weren't any closer to finding any documentation or information about Ephraim's magical potion.

A fellow Harvard student had heard about his classmates' midnight escapade into the burial ground, and he himself doubted a man really had been entombed in Ephraim's coffin. He decided to take a solitary sojourn to the burial ground on a cloudy and blustery night. He entered the tomb alone, lit a lantern and then unpacked a saw from his bag. He had decided that he would saw the head off the body so that he could take it home and examine it at his leisure. With a strong stomach, he proceeded to saw the head off the body, and just as he finished his gruesome task, he heard strange noises.

He heard the sound of whispers coming from the dark corners of the tomb. Outside of the tomb, he could hear footsteps on the wet grass, and they sounded like they were coming closer. The whispers soon turned into moans, wails and steady cries. The frightened student looked toward the mossy door to the tomb and saw strange shapes in the shadows moving closer toward him and across the green, slimy walls. The once-brave student yelled out for mercy. With a sickening thud, he flung the head onto the floor and ran out of the tomb. He tripped over grave markers and stones with every frenzied step as he made his way across the burial ground. He didn't turn to look behind him but ran home as fast as his legs would carry him.

Many months passed before anyone else summoned enough courage to go into the tomb. Adventurous boys would dare their friends to go into the tomb and look for Ephraim's missing head. One day, however, a man who was bathing in the river just before sunrise saw something that changed his life—and it came out of Ephraim's tomb. The man ran through the streets of Malden screaming that a white-robed figure had emerged from the tomb. It was soon determined that the figure was not a corpse but an insane man who had crawled into Ephraim's house of death to sleep. The bathing man had been so frightened by seeing the strange specter that he refused to believe that what he saw was actually a live human being. He claimed to have been summoned by a ghost that day and that the sighting was an omen of his death. From that point on, the man began to change. He became silent and self-absorbed, and it wasn't long until he was dead.

By the early 1900s, the population of Malden had grown significantly, and it was decided that a road needed to be constructed where the old burial ground was. A decision was made to disinter the bodies and reinter them at a new burying location in the city. Things were going well for the workers until they started to dismantle Ephraim Gray's mausoleum. The roof and the walls dismantled easily enough; however, when the coffin was lifted, it was found to be unusually light. Workers decided to open the coffin on the spot, and when the lid was taken off, the coffin was discovered to be empty. Had Ephraim finally awakened from his slumber? Had he perhaps gone to search for his head? The rest of the old burial ground ended up being moved, but the remains of Ephraim Gray were never found.

GRAVE ROBBING IN THE NAME OF SCIENCE, SPRINGFIELD

A grisly grave robbery took place in Springfield, Massachusetts, around the scenic Pioneer Valley in the western part of the state. This disturbing event took place between 1826 and 1830, and the complete details were documented in a dusty old scrapbook of newspaper articles that were written by Dr. Alfred and kept in the city library. Alfred was a reporter for the *Republican*, a local Springfield newspaper. The account discussed the unorthodox practices of Dr. W.L. Loring. Dr. Loring was educated at Harvard Medical College, but despite his top-notch education, the good doctor did not have a successful practice. Desperate for a solid source of income, Dr. Loring found an ambitious way to make fast money with some help from the dead, and the tale of how he made his income struck readers with unimaginable terror.

The Pittsfield Medical College in Pittsfield, Massachusetts, had trouble obtaining bodies for dissection. Dr. Loring undertook a scheme to supply the demand of the growing school by furnishing crematory remains, skeletons and, whenever possible, complete bodies. On the morning of February 25, 1826, curious people quickly gathered in the Old Burial Ground, which was located at the foot of Elm Street. The sight of the empty and unfilled grave of Jonathan M. Moulthrop sent a nervous chill throughout the community. Just a few days earlier, Moulthrop had committed suicide by hanging himself. Moulthrop was a healthy person, so his corpse was quite desirable to those who were looking to learn more about the human body. According to the account, the body was discovered near the home of Dr. Loring by the armory, and while many people suspected that the doctor had removed the body from the grave, there were no witnesses.

It wasn't long before some citizens became vigilant protectors of the recently deceased. Groups of people would hide out in the cemeteries and watch for anyone who looked suspicious. One group of three young men watched over the grave of Mrs. Hamilton of Chicopee Falls. The men were concerned because Mrs. Hamilton had killed herself in a crazy fit and little damage was done to her body. One night, Dr. Loring and two of his students, Mr. Whitman and Jacob Perkins Jr., approached the grave and were unaware that they were being watched until one of the spies shouted out, "What do you want there?" The doctor feared that he might be caught and fled with his two accomplices. However, a few days later, the doctor and his ghoulish henchmen visited the grave once again, and when they discovered that there was no one around, Mrs. Hamilton's body was stolen out of the grave.

It was after this incident that the general public became so fearful that they did not want to bury the dead. Then there was the case with the body of Mrs. Russell Curtis, a woman who, in a fit of insanity, committed suicide. Mrs. Russell's family and friends knew that her body would be a target, and they decided not to bury her. It had become apparent that Dr. Loring was seeking suicide victims. Once the funeral at the old Methodist church on Union Street was over, Mrs. Russell's body was removed and brought to the home of friends. Residents in the area described seeing three suspicious characters hovering around the house and believed that they were Pittsfield medical students. Fearful that the body would be stolen, Mrs. Russell's friends moved her again. Her body was placed in the basement of the Methodist church for what was described as a "long time." The final resting place of Mrs. Russell's body is unknown.

It wasn't long before another grave was robbed from the Old Burial Ground on Elm Street. The body of William Nevers had disappeared. There was such an outcry at this point that the matter came before the city's selectmen. An investigation followed, and Dr. Loring, Jacob Perkins Jr. and George Ball were finally arrested. William Nevers's body had been found in Westfield before it could be transferred to Pittsfield. After the arrests, it was decided that a tomb should be built in order to protect the dead.

Dr. Loring's trial took place in May 1819. Residents of the community waited anxiously to hear what his fate would be. Perkins was fined just $50, and Dr. Loring was fined $500. Amazingly, the governor's council felt that Dr. Loring's work was not "wholly unworthy."

After the trial, residents were still suspicious of Dr. Loring, and they continued to blame him for strange occurrences over the next couple of years. A thirteen-year-old girl living near the city park in West Springfield told a frightening tale that was associated with Dr. Loring. She said that she awoke at 1:00 a.m. and found herself in the arms of a strange man who was carrying her from her bedroom through the back part of the house and around to the outside gate of the yard. When she came to her senses, she struggled and jumped from the stranger's arms. The stranger then attempted to strangle her to silence her screams. Then suddenly, he dropped her, and she managed to run back to the house. When she ran inside, she found her father preparing to pursue the invader. Everyone in the neighborhood combed through the area that night looking for the girl's attacker, but he was never found. An investigation ensued, and three persons, one of whom was Dr. Loring, were brought before the girl for identification. She claimed that he was the guilty one but did not make the statement with absolute certainty of truth. Dr. Loring's reputation soon spread beyond the town's limits. According to one of the articles, a young boy who lived in Wilbraham was so frightened of being abducted that every night during the winter, he poured water around the window casings and sash so that the ice would prevent Dr. Loring from opening the windows and carrying the boy or some of his family away.

The scrapbook included specific quotes by Dr. Booth about Dr. Loring, such as this one: "An anatomist who with all his Band of rude disciples over the subject hung And impolitely hewed his way through bones And muscles of the sacred human form Exposing barbarously to wanton gaze the mysteries of nature. Chill penury repressed his noble rage, And froze the genial current of his soul."

Dr. Loring's reputation finally destroyed his practice, and his family suffered from poverty. His wife received a lot of sympathy from some of the women in town who believed that she was a woman of many good qualities. According to the reports about her, she had often been compelled to sleep in a bed with dead bodies hidden underneath. Eventually the doctor disappeared from the area, leaving his wife and three children behind. She later married a clergyman, and her family moved to another part of the country.

The Old Burial Ground on Elm Street had grown so overcrowded by 1848 that the city made the decision to remove all of the 2,434 bodies and move them to Peabody Cemetery. Some of the empty graves that were discovered during that move were rumored to be victims of the famous grave robbers Dr. Loring and his henchmen.

BROOKFIELD CEMETERY

Located in Worcester County is the quiet little town of Brookfield. Historic Brookfield Cemetery is home to a noted collection of gravestones from the 1700s that depict carvings of colonial faces surrounded by triangles, swirls and vines. The grave for Lieutenant Josiah Hamilton features a face surrounded by a halo of stars, and the borders of the stone have long trailing grapevines. The stone for Robert Cutler, who died in 1761, depicts the portrait of a man with two doves alighting on his shoulders. A stone for Sarah Moore, who died in 1781, depicts a smiling woman surrounded by fan-sized leaves. The gravestone for Elizabeth and Ayres Putnam is believed to have been carved by William Young and depicts two faces, one large and one small.

Probably one of the most famous graves in the burying ground is for Joshua Spooner. The inscription on the stone reads:

Joshua Spooner Murdered Mar. 1, 1778 by three soldiers of the Revolution
Ross, Brooks, and Buchanan at the instigation of his wife Bathsheba
They were all executed at Worcester July 2, 1778

Joshua's wife, Bathsheba, was the daughter of General Timothy Ruggles, who was one of the highest-ranking officers during the French and Indian War. A Boston newspaper called the *Massachusetts Spy* (also known as the *American Oracle of Liberty*) chronicled the tale in its May 7, 1778 edition:

It appeared by the course of the evidence, that Mrs. Spooner had, for some time, conceived a great aversion to her husband, with whom she had lived about 14 years: His only fault appears to be his not supporting a manly importance as head of his family, and not regulating the government of it. It is very uncertain what this aversion in Mrs. Spooner's mind at first arose from, but from the general tenor of her conduct, it is probable that she cherished a criminal regard for some other persons, until having followed the blind impulses of wicked and unchaste desire, she left all moral sensibility, discarded reason and conscience from her breast, and gave herself up to infamous prostitutions, and finally became determined to destroy the life of her husband, who seemed to check her wanton career in no other way then by preventing her wasting his whole estate as she pleased[.] In pursuance of this horrid design, she at various times, procured poison, but never gave it to him; and sometime before the commission of this cruel fact, she became acquainted with [Ezra] Ross, to whom she made some amorous overtures, and told him, that if he would kill her husband, she would become his lawful wife. It appears, by the examination of Ross, before the Justices, that his conscience at first started at the appearance of so much guilt; but upon her persuasions and the fancied happiness of marrying a woman so much above his rank in life, and the allurements of wallowing in Mr. Spooner's wealth, he fatally consented.

Mrs. Spooner[,] tired with the delays of Ross, made like overtures to Sergeant Buchanan…whom she directed to be called in, as he was passing on the road. Buchanan and she engaged one William Brooks, of the same troops, to commit the murder, promising him the deceased's watch, buckles, and a thousand dollars.

Bathsheba conspired with the three men, and they laid in wait one night for Ezra to come home. When he arrived, they beat him to death and threw his body down a well. Within twenty-four hours of her husband's death, the authorities were investigating the situation. It didn't take long for the three men to confess and implicate Bathsheba in the crime. The case quickly went to trial, and all four conspirators were found guilty and sentenced to death by hanging. Bathsheba tried to get a stay of execution because she was five months pregnant at the time; her appeal, however, was denied, and she was executed along with the three men on July 2, 1778, in front of almost five thousand people. The telling gravestone in Brookfield Cemetery was believed to have been commissioned about fifty years after Ezra's death by a relative. Bathsheba was buried in an unmarked grave in the area that is now known as Green Hill Park in Worcester.

Chapter Seven
Unearthing the Ghosts

THE TALE OF LUCY KEYES, PRINCETON

A winding road alongside Mount Wachusett leads visitors to the Old Meetinghouse Burial Ground in Princeton, Massachusetts, which is the setting of a truly tragic tale. Generations of townspeople have told the story of little Lucy Keyes. Robert Keyes purchased nearly two hundred acres of property at the foot of Mount Wachusett in 1751, and his family was one of the first to settle in the area. A blacksmith by trade, Robert soon became a skilled huntsman in this very wild and unsettled land. His house was built near what was then known as the Old Indian Trail.

There were ten children born into the Keyes family. On April 14, 1755, Lucy Keyes, age four years and eight months, went with her two sisters into the woods to fetch some sand from Wachusett Lake to bring back to their house. At some point, Lucy wandered away from her sisters and became lost. Every able-bodied person for nearly thirty miles around Princeton gathered to search for Lucy. They trudged through the forest for days and weeks but could not find a trace of the little girl. Efforts were even made to drag the pond numerous times for any sign of her. All of their pursuits and efforts were in vain: Lucy Keyes was never found. Her mother, Martha, refused to give up hope, and it was said that she would venture into the woods for hours, crying, "Lucy—Luuucy!" Many of the townspeople thought Martha had been driven to the verge of insanity in her desperate search for her lost child. Rumors that Lucy had been taken captive by Indians only added to Martha's despair.

Ten years after Lucy's disappearance, her father petitioned the General Court of the Province of Massachusetts for support. He explained his family's

The woods adjacent to the Old Meetinghouse Burial Ground in Princeton are said to be as haunted as the burial ground itself.

desperate and costly efforts to find Lucy and requested assistance, as he was finding it difficult to afford the maintenance of his home and land. The petition was rejected, and he ended up selling most of his property so that his family could survive. Mrs. Martha Keyes died August 9, 1789, and her husband died March 1, 1795. They are both buried in the Old Meetinghouse Burial Ground.

Shortly after the deaths of Martha and Robert, two men from Groton, Massachusetts, returned from a trip to Canada and claimed to have met a white woman living with Indians there who matched Lucy's description. They stated that she knew nothing of her name or family, but she remembered that she lived near "'Chusett Hill." Even more strange than the story of their alleged encounter was a letter that was found that described in gruesome detail the murder of little Lucy Keyes. The letter was from Tilly Littlejohn and was believed to have been written on his deathbed. Tilly claimed to be Keyes's neighbor and wrote that, one day, he had a dispute with Robert Keyes over the boundaries of their property lines. A heated argument followed, and Tilly sought his revenge when he found Lucy in the woods. He confessed to killing her by hitting her head on a fallen tree and then stuffing her body inside a hollow log. He waited until nightfall to dig a hole and bury the body at the base of an uprooted tree. The search party had found a lock of hair in the vicinity of where he said he had killed Lucy, and the family had identified the hair as Lucy's. Tilly became nervous that the murder might be uncovered, so he decided to leave the area. The strange letter did inspire some questions, as the facts did not seem to add up, creating more confusion and speculation.

The grave for Martha Keyes is easy to find in the cemetery and is decorated with tokens of remembrance. Beads, pennies, ribbon and even a little ceramic lamb are some of the mementos left by those who still acknowledge Martha's pain and never-ending mourning for her lost child. A number of people have reported seeing Martha's spirit, which only reminds visitors/locals of the story of little Lucy. Visitors to the cemetery have claimed to hear a woman's voice calling, "Lucy!" An apparition of a woman dressed in colonial clothing has also reportedly been seen wandering about the woods and cemetery.

During the shooting of a Lifetime Channel movie based on the story of Lucy Keyes, the cast and crew reported numerous instances of unusual activity. Photographs revealed strange mists around Martha's grave, and local paranormal groups that reviewed the photos thought that they showed a portal or a doorway between our world and the spirit world. In some of these photos, there was an image of a woman who seemed to be passing through the portal. Other photos show vapors and what is thought to be spiritual energy in the graveyard. One curious photo was of a man wearing a priest's cloak and a broad brimmed hat standing with a book in his hands by the stone wall in the back of the cemetery.

Those who work at the nearby Wachusett Mountain Ski Area tell stories of hearing strange sounds and seeing unexplained shadows on the mountain. One tale describes seeing fresh child-size footprints in the snow at two o'clock in the morning, when no one else was around. The mystery of Lucy Keyes's disappearance continues to intrigue the Princeton Historical Society. It has Lucy's cradle in its collection of antique artifacts, and it has documented the ghost stories from visitors to the mountain as well.

The peaceful atmosphere of this old burial ground is broken by a lingering sadness there, and one cannot help but be compelled to look into the adjacent woods and contemplate Lucy's fate. Does the spirit of Martha Keyes still tread the mossy grove of this burial ground? Are her plaintive cries still echoing in the woods? Some say one visit will make you a believer.

In addition to Martha's grave, there are a number of other interesting headstones in the burial ground. Two gravestones of interest belong to Africans Thomas and Flova, who were "Negro" servants interred in the cemetery in 1783 and 1778, respectively. These stones feature unique carvings of faces with African features and hair. Most servants during this time were buried in unmarked graves, making these stones quite unusual. In another part of the cemetery, a rather simple slate stone with an angel reads: "In memory of Capt. Elisha Allen who was inhumanly murdered by Samuel Frost July 16th, 1793 aged 48 years." The *Massachusetts Spy* detailed the crime in its July 22, 1793 edition:

> *Captain Allen had left his house in order to set out some cabbage plants at a little distance, and ordered Frost, who lived with him several years, to go with him. Having proceeded a little way, he recollected he wanted a hoe, sent Frost back to get one, and himself went on, and began his work. Frost returned with the hoe, and is supposed, got over the fence behind the Captain, who probably stooping down, struck him on the head with the edge of the hoe, which knocked him down, after which he continued his blows until he had bruised his head to pieces in the most shocking manner.*

Samuel Frost was not new to the court system; in fact, he had been previously tried for murdering his father. However, he was deemed insane at the time and released. Samuel later confessed to the murder of Captain Allen, and he described that he felt like he was worked too hard and was treated like a slave. Samuel was sentenced to be hanged on November 6, 1793. The sheriff who was present at the hanging said that Samuel wanted the execution to happen on time, as he was "ready to go." Two thousand people witnessed Samuel's execution. The gravestone for Captain Allen serves as a chilling reminder of his gruesome death.

Near the gate to the burial ground are two tombs, including the town tomb. The doors to them are missing and are now bricked shut. Small holes can be found in the crumbling brickwork, allowing the morbidly curious a glimpse into the gloom of the crypt with a flashlight or camera. The tombs do not disappoint curiosity seekers, as bones are strewn across the floor amidst deteriorating bricks. Strangely, there are no skulls to be found.

As the sun sets each day over this cemetery, the truth behind the murder and mysteries of Princeton's past slips further into the shadows and the past of Mount Wachusett.

HOWARD STREET CEMETERY, SALEM

In Salem, Massachusetts, the tragedies of the 1692 witch trials are intertwined with modern-day commercialism. Ghost tours shuffle visitors from place to place, and on every corner, there are shops that offer fortune-telling services to the inquisitive. Salem is a city that has long been a destination for those

Does the spirit of Giles Corey still wander Howard Street Cemetery in Salem?

fascinated with this dark chapter from New England's history. The grounds of Howard Street Cemetery are linked to the city's infamous past.

Giles Corey was one of six men who were executed during the Salem witch hysteria. Giles was eighty years old and was married to Martha Corey, who was also tried and put to death for practicing witchcraft. Giles maintained his innocence and pled not guilty, and he even refused to be tried in court, as he felt the jury was already predisposed to deliver a guilty verdict. Many people speculated that Corey refused to stand trial because he was afraid his land would be taken, while others believed that he refused out of sheer rebellion.

Sheriff George Corwin and his deputies brought Giles out to a pit in a grassy field and forced him to lay down. A door was placed over Giles, and large rocks were piled up on top of it to press a "confession" out of him. Giles refused to confess, and near the end of the second day, Giles answered his tormenters by asking for more weight. His body quickly responded: his eyes bulged, and his tongue popped out of his mouth. Sheriff Corwin pushed Giles's tongue back in with his cane. With his dying breath, Giles cursed the sheriff and the town of Salem. His body was left in a pit on the grounds.

The curse of Giles Corey has come true, according to Robert Cahill, a local historian and former sheriff of Essex County. Cahill has spent a lot of time chronicling the town's history following Corey's curse. When Robert was interviewed by the History Channel, he pointed out that each sheriff from George Corwin to himself had either died in office or was forced into early retirement due to a heart or blood ailment.

In 1801, the Howard Street Cemetery was opened. Benjamin Ropes was the first person to be buried there, on August 5, 1801. Benjamin was a second mate on the ship *Belisarius*, and he was crushed to death while launching its foretopmast. Another early grave in the cemetery belongs to Captain William Browne. He was the commander of the ship *Brutus*, which sailed from Salem on February 21, 1802, and was wrecked on the shores of Cape Cod, along with two other Salem-based ships, *Ulysses* and *Volusia*, during a violent nor'easter the following day. Captain Browne and many of his crew made it to shore but died of exposure. Many people speculate that he is not actually interred in Salem, despite the fact that his gravestone is in the cemetery. It is believed that his remains are actually buried somewhere on Cape Cod near Provincetown.

Various war veterans can also be found in Howard Street Cemetery, including Colonel Samuel Carlton, who, with a company he raised himself, marched to Ticonderoga, New York. The colonel was also at Valley Forge with George Washington. A small white marble gravestone with a shield is for George W. Beatty, who was a Union army veteran with the Twenty-eighth Massachusetts Infantry.

Also buried here is George Ropes, who died in 1819. Ropes was a renowned local artist who painted views of Salem Harbor. There are many interesting carvings on the stones in the cemetery. Among them are a setting sun and Roman numerals on the gravestone for Mary Baker, who was only one year and six months old at the time of her death. Part of the cemetery was designated for Africans, and another section was designated for "strangers"; those areas remain unmarked on the grounds today.

Looming ominously at the edge of the cemetery is the old Salem Jail, which was built in 1811. One of the oldest correctional facilities in the country, it was vacated in 1991 and has recently been renovated and turned into condominiums. However, the structure still casts an ominous dark shadow across the grounds.

Howard Street Cemetery is the place where the ghost of Giles Corey is most often seen. There is no marker that shows the location of his burial, and it's uncertain where on the grounds his remains are. In 1914, Salem residents reported seeing the ghost of Giles at the cemetery just before a great fire broke out that same year. Coincidentally, the Great Fire of 1914 began on Gallows Hill, where nineteen witches were hanged. Visitors to the cemetery often capture strange phenomena on their camera phones, including ghostly shapes.

SAGAMORE CEMETERY, BOURNE

You can't ignore the story of the ghosts in Sagamore Cemetery, located on Route 6A in Bourne, Massachusetts, which is known as the gateway to Cape Cod. Bordered by Plymouth and Wareham, Bourne was occupied by English colonists as early as 1627. The burial ground is spacious and features a gnarly old tree that looks as though it has swallowed several bodies over the years due to its eerily fascinating shape. Stories of the ghosts that inhabit this graveyard have been published in local papers and have also been featured in Boston television news broadcasts. The first burial recorded in Sagamore Cemetery was in 1803, and most of the gravestones here date back to the nineteenth century.

There are many who reside here that were removed from the old Bournedale Cemetery. Apparently, there was a bit of confusion when laborers dug up the dead and took the remains to Sagamore. New coffins were built for many of the bodies that were being moved to Sagamore by Keith Car Works, a local manufacturer of boxcars. Unfortunately, the wrong headstones were placed over some of the disinterred remains. The remains of the Bourne family themselves were part of the upheaval in the burial ground. Their graves were displaced to make way for construction of the Cape Cod Canal. The family included Captain Elisha Bourne (1733–1804), who was banished to Rhode Island during the Revolutionary War for being a Tory. Captain Bourne was only allowed to return home under an act of the legislature. After Captain Bourne passed away, his body was also buried in old Bournedale Cemetery, which was quickly becoming the resting place for many of the prominent families of the area. The mix-up of the moved remains has only contributed to the number of ghost stories that are told by local residents.

The burial ground is the final resting place of Isaac Keith, a local businessman, who reportedly has haunted the grounds for many years. Some folks think that Keith's spirit might be still wandering because of the grave mix-up. Psychics believe that the spirit of Captain Elisha Bourne may also be disturbed about the misplaced graves. Several people have reported feeling an icy grip around their bodies, and many others have reported seeing a man in a top hat wandering the grounds, only to disappear when someone approaches. Other visitors claim to have captured strange images of bright orbs and shadowy figures on camera.

There is a fantastic story about a gravestone moving off its base on its own. A large marble stone was completely off its foundation one day, and there was no sign showing that it had been pried off. Donald Ellis, the caretaker, was so disturbed by the moved stone that he called the police. But there was no evidence of vandals, and Ellis and the police gave up trying to figure it out.

Emory Ellis (no relation to Donald) was a big, cigar-smoking man, who lived in the early part of the twentieth century. His family had a plot in Sagamore Cemetery that was in the path of new construction. State officials ordered the plot and its inhabitants be moved, but Emory would have none of it. He even kept the men at bay with a shovel and a shotgun when the state tried to move the burial ground. Eventually, he was offered enough money, and he backed down and allowed his ancestors to be moved elsewhere on the grounds. But to this day, the smell of cigar smoke is prevalent in the cemetery, and some believe old Emory's spirit is still upset about his ancestors' remains being moved.

Local ghost tours bring thrill seekers to Sagamore Cemetery who hope to catch a glimpse of the ghosts of the past. Some visitors have run out of the cemetery claiming to have sensed an unseen presence behind them.

The Warning from beyond the Grave, Nahant

Originally part of Lynn, the town of Nahant is a peninsula located in the southernmost part of Essex County. The town was settled in the early 1600s, and early residents made their living from fishing and farming. All of the original trees that stood in the area were cleared under a mandate issued in 1657. Visitors to the area were attracted to the town and its unique location, and it wasn't long before it became a tourist colony.

It was around the year 1815 that a family came from Medford to summer in Nahant. The family took up residence in a little ocean cottage next to one owned by an Italian family. A young lady from the Medford family named Alice was enjoying her stay, and she soon met a young man named Faustino, who lived in the cottage next door. The two got along wonderfully and spent much of their time beachcombing and climbing on the rocks to watch the waves. At the end of the summer, the couple announced their happy engagement. However, they couldn't move ahead with their plans until they each had parental consent. Faustino's parents were away in Livorno, Italy, so Faustino made his way to Boston, where he made plans to sail to Italy.

The day before Faustino was to leave America, the couple spent the afternoon sitting on the ledges across from an island called Egg Rock. The romantic notion came to young Faustino to make one final gesture to prove his love to Alice before he made the long voyage to Italy. There was a local legend at the time that if a young lady received a bouquet of forget-me-not flowers that grew on Egg Rock, she and her loved one would remain true forever.

With that thought, Faustino stood up on the rocks, smiled and made his way to the boat. Alice pleaded with him that it wasn't necessary, and she didn't have a good feeling. Faustino wanted to show his courage and proceeded to the beach to get his boat as a light wind started to blow. He was cautioned by a man about taking the boat out on the beach. The man suggested that Faustino should wait until the next tide. Faustino told him that he wouldn't be able to wait until the next tide, as that one was going to be the one he sailed for Italy on.

Faustino climbed in the boat and waved a farewell to his anxious sweetheart who stood on the shore. The boat tumbled gently over the waves to Egg Rock, which was about a mile out. When he reached the island, he climbed up the rocks and found the nook where the forget-me-nots grew. He grasped a handful of the flowers and started to make his way back down to the boat as the winds began to pick up. The ride across the water to Nahant had become more treacherous; wind and waves caused the boat to struggle against the fast-rising tide, and Faustino found that he couldn't navigate back to the beach where he had first cast off. Soon, the crashing waves were breaking almost ten feet high.

Alice stood on the windswept cliff where she and Faustino had just sat a little while before and watched the frightening events unfold. A huge wave engulfed the sailboat and tossed it mercilessly against the rocky cliffs. The young man looked up at Alice for just a moment, and then he and his boat were gone under the waves.

Alice was carried back to her cottage, as she had collapsed on the cliff. The very next morning, local fishermen knocked on the door and escorted her down to the beach. Faustino's body had washed ashore on the beach connecting Nahant and Lynn. A crowd had gathered around the body, and when the blanket that covered him was removed, Alice cried out in horror. His hand was still clenched around the flowers that he had gathered for her from Egg Rock. She bent down, took one of the flowers, turned and made her way back to the beach cottage. Alice was so grief-stricken that she fell ill later that day. Her family then returned to Medford, and for the rest of that winter, she became withdrawn and, in fact, never even walked again. Alice remained in a deep state of mourning until the following spring, when she finally died. She was buried in the family plot in Medford, and those who visited her grave over the next 150 years said that it was quite haunted. Whenever the winds begin to rise, cries of "Faustino! Faustino!" can be heard coming up from her grave.

THE GRAVE OF JOHN HAYS HAMMOND, MAGNOLIA

John Hays Hammond Jr. was a true Renaissance man. He was inventive, imaginative and, most of all, resourceful. As a little boy, he visited Thomas Edison's laboratory with his wealthy father, the South African diamond mining

John Hays Hammond was disinterred from his original burial site, and the land where he once laid was sold in order to keep the castle open to the public.

Hammond Castle is home to the grave of John Hays Hammond, and it is believed his ghost still walks the grounds.

magnate John Hays Hammond Sr. The young Hammond pestered Edison with so many questions that Edison took him under his wing and acted as his mentor. The two remained friends until Edison's death.

Hammond would indeed follow in the inventor's prolific footsteps and become second to Edison himself for the most invention patents filed. John Hays Hammond Jr. had created over eight hundred inventions, and he held 426 patents in the fields of radio, television and radar. Hammond served on the board of RCA and did significant work on remote control via radio waves, earning him the title "the father of remote control."

A passionate traveler, Hammond had a deep love of all things European and historic. In a letter to a friend, he wrote:

> *For the last three days I motored many miles through Europe. After traveling all day, I would arrive at my destination to see a church, a cathedral, a town hall, a scrap of Roman wall or viaduct, a coliseum or ancient theater. It was always a piece of architecture that suddenly dissipated the obscurity of time and brought the living presence back of all ages. It is in the stones and wood that the personal record of man comes down to us. We call it atmosphere, this indescribable something that still haunts old monuments. You can read history, you can visit a hundred museums containing their handiwork, but nothing can reincarnate their spirit except to walk through rooms in which they have lived and through the scenes that were the background of their lives. It is a marvelous thing, this expression of human ideals in walls and windows.*

Hammond certainly expressed himself in the walls and windows of his New England home—a medieval-style castle complete with a drawbridge, which he dubbed "Abbadia Mare." It was built between 1926 and 1929 on a steep hill overlooking the Atlantic Ocean in Gloucester, Massachusetts. The castle is divided into four sections, each epitomizing a style in European architectural history: Romanesque, Medieval, Gothic and Renaissance. Some of the architectural details include a round library, a basement war room and even an indoor pool with a lifesize nude, bronze statue of Hammond. The courtyard where the pool resides has a "weather control" system that was installed so that Hammond could set it whenever he felt like swimming in the rain. The castle was an expression of all things that Hammond loved, and his behavior showed it. A joyous Hammond was known to leap cannonball style from a second-story window into his courtyard pool.

Fascinating artifacts can be found in Hammond's home, which is now a museum. There is a fifteenth-century skull of one of the mariners who sailed with none other than Christopher Columbus. Hammond felt that he, too, was an explorer and that he should honor the spirit of an explorer who came before him by placing his skull in his home. In some ways, he thought that he could connect with his spirit and gain inspiration.

There are relics around every corner of the castle that have unusual connections to the dead and the spirit world. There is a real marble sarcophagus of a child from second-century Rome that is on display. There are also ancient Roman tombstones within the stone walls that are thousands of years old. Above most of the innumerable doorways and many windows are hundreds of expressive gargoyles within the stonework. A labyrinth of hidden passageways and secret doors are hidden behind the looming walls of the castle. Some of the more massive doors in the castle are thousands of years old and were brought over from Europe. Each had its own fascinating history; many of them are authentic medieval dungeon doors. In fact, the castle has its very own dungeon tower complete with a large collection of medieval weapons.

The great hall is one of the most impressive rooms in the castle with its sixty-foot ceiling and ornate stained-glass window. At one side of the room is an incredible pipe organ with 8,200 pipes—the largest organ ever installed in a private home. The great hall was one of Hammond's favorite places to entertain. In fact, he would often stage Shakespearean plays in the hall and invite people such as George Gershwin, Cole Porter, John D. Rockefeller and Ethel and Lionel Barrymore.

Hammond was an avid Spiritualist who believed in the paranormal, and séances were regularly held at the castle. He even conducted a number of psychic experiments at the castle with Eileen Garrett, one of the twentieth century's most prestigious mediums and psychic researchers. Hammond set out to prove that psychic energy really existed, and he also hoped to enhance it, if possible. During one of the experiments at the castle, he constructed a Faraday cage to isolate Eileen. (Faraday cages were designed in the nineteenth century to block electromagnetic waves so that undisturbed paranormal research could be conducted.) According to local legend, it may have been during this experiment that a spot on the floor of the Great Hall was bleached out by psychic energies.

Before John Hays Hammond died in 1965, he had his burial tomb built. The tomb was designed in an ancient Aztec style, and it looked much like another worldly antique artifact when it was completed. Hammond liked to go outdoors, sit on the top of the tomb and have lunch on a regular basis. He enjoyed bringing visitors out to tour the tomb before he died, and people were quite surprised to see that the locks to the tomb door were on the inside rather than the outside. After Hammond's death, he was entombed as he had wished along the border to the property. However, due to financial difficulties, the organization that operates the castle had to sell the land where John was entombed in 2008. John Hays Hammond was disinterred from his tomb against his wishes and reinterred in the courtyard garden at the back of the castle.

Some people believe that perhaps John's spirit has returned to the property as a black cat that roams the grounds. It was common knowledge that he wanted to be reincarnated as a cat, as he was completely fascinated by them. Often, he would take in cats that came on to his property, and when they died, he had them preserved in formaldehyde. He even named one of his cats "Boo." In fact, John was originally interred with some of his Siamese cats' remains. A stray cat once frequented the stone bishop's chair that Hammond liked to sit and smoke in, and guests touring the castle have reported feeling a small animal brush up against their legs. Many who have visited Hammond's tomb have also claimed to have heard the muffled sounds of crying cats when none is present.

The fascinating circular library was one of Hammond's favorite places, and he spent a lot of time in there while he was alive. He owned an extensive collection of books on the occult and spirits. Many caretakers have reported finding these books left open and lying on the desk or carelessly thrown onto the couches and chairs. Disembodied voices are often heard in the library, as well as throughout the rest of the castle.

One of the spirits is believed to be that of Hammond's wife, Irene Fenton, whom he had secretly married in 1926. Irene was quite depressed in the great castle, and she gradually became reclusive and unhappy in marriage. Irene was an accomplished artist, and she painted the walls of her bedroom with colorful scenes of animals, trees and flowers. Then she painted a wide railing over the scene to show how trapped she truly felt. Irene is often seen gazing out of a window of the Italian villa that overlooks the indoor pool.

The ghosts that wander the lonesome halls of the house turned museum make their presence known on a regular basis. A ghostly shadow man has often been seen in the organ loft, even when the door to the loft is closed and locked. The pipe organ in the Great Hall has been known to mysteriously play itself as well.

The castle is often the setting for fairy tale weddings. These weddings are often attended by unknown and uninvited figures that circulate among the guests, vanishing when anyone tries to get close to them, and they have even shown up in wedding photographs. Many people believe that there are two reasons why the castle and grounds are so haunted. One theory is that Hammond's belief in Spiritualism was so strong that he has returned to prove that there is life beyond the grave. Others believe that since Hammond was disinterred and placed in a simple grave against his wishes, his spirit cannot rest.

OLD NORTH CEMETERY, TRURO

Located on the quiet end of Route 6 in Truro is the Old North Cemetery, once known as the Burying Acre. The cemetery's first burial took place in 1713. The sandy grounds are clear and wide open with very few trees or shrubs in the cemetery. The hill that the cemetery is on was known throughout the eighteenth and nineteenth centuries as the "Hill of Storms." The townspeople had built their meetinghouse at the top of the hill, which had a splendid view down into the village. Deacon Collins was one of the men who helped to raise the meetinghouse; he even helped to split and chop the wood. He always made sure that he sat in a position in the church where he could get a good view of all of the parishioners so that he could wake them up should they dare to fall asleep during a sermon.

The deacon was always concerned with making sure that he transported the sacramental wine for Sabbath services on time to the meetinghouse. At times, his old horse didn't move quickly enough for the deacon, and he shouted and flailed at it as they trod up the hill. Often, the deacon overexcited himself and his horse, too, as he was always the first to arrive to the meetinghouse, far before any of his parishioners.

One spring, the townsfolk of Truro had to deal with the sad return of a ship that had survived a calamity known as the Seven Ways Gale. The gale shifted the boat seven different ways against the tide, smashing the mast of the ship to pieces. The vessel was owned by a man named Henry Rich, and he had his young son, Silas, on board with him. Silas was well known and loved by the community, and he was forever telling everyone how he couldn't wait to take a voyage out at

A fieldstone marker from 1741 can be found in Old North Cemetery in Truro.

sea with his father. The people were heartbroken when they learned that Silas was tangled in the ship's rigging and dragged into the water during the storm. A wave threw him back on the boat, but the boy's head collided with the ship's gear, and he lost his memory. He was no longer the same boy everyone had known. His speech and memory seemed slower, and he appeared disabled and his body moved strangely when he walked. The asylums on the Lower Cape would not take the boy in, and he became a responsibility of the town.

Silas was a good young man, and he was well liked by everyone. Sometimes, he would be found out wandering in the dunes, and the townsmen would have to walk him back home. He went to church every Sunday and sat quietly during services. The townspeople seemed to have patience for the poor, unfortunate boy, and they always used gentle words with him.

The following year, Deacon Collins was preparing the materials needed for Sabbath services, and once again, he was in a rush. He worried that the Lord would look on him with disfavor if he did not deliver them on time. The deacon mounted his horse and showered kicks and blows against the nag to get her to move quickly. The tired horse sped up the hill but, unfortunately, slipped in the sand. The wine almost fell off the horse, and the deacon could barely hold on himself. Trying to regain control, he didn't see Silas directly in his path. The horse charged into the young boy and knocked him to the ground. The deacon was in such a frenzy that he almost didn't even notice what had just happened. The horse's hooves even nicked a few gravestones before it finally stopped in the cemetery. The deacon arrived at the meetinghouse, early as usual; however, coming right after him were a few men of the town who were carrying the body of young Silas. The boy never opened his eyes again. The townspeople turned away from the deacon, unable to look at him, and the deacon himself realized what he had done. One of the goodmen of the town took to speaking to the crowd, while the deacon took one last look at Silas and walked out of the meetinghouse. The townsfolk elected the goodman the new deacon, and the former Deacon Collins never attended another service.

When he died, the deacon was buried on the hill, as was Silas. Those who remembered the story said that the impression of the horse's hooves never disappeared from the burial ground until the former deacon was dead. They said that his spirit could not rest in heaven and you can still see him in the burial ground on the first Sunday of the month, when the moon is out at midnight. According to the story, he descends from heaven and rides through the Hill of Storms to visit Silas's grave. And there he prays all night until dawn, when he rides his horse back to heaven. Evidence of his visit can be seen by viewing the horseshoe marks on the grounds.

Chapter Eight

Finding the Lost
and Forgotten

DANVERS STATE HOSPITAL CEMETERY, DANVERS

The cemeteries of Danvers State Hospital are almost as legendary as the old asylum itself. A large memorial boulder that stands near the entrance to one of the cemeteries reads, "The Danvers State Hospital Cemetery, the Echoes They Left Behind." Once known as the "Castle on the Hill," Danvers State Hospital held frightening memories for many people because of what the facility ended up becoming in its last fifty years.

Construction began in 1874, and the facility, known as the State Lunatic Hospital at Danvers, opened in 1878. The campus was designed in the Kirkbride plan (a plan to build asylums advocated by Philadelphia psychiatrist Thomas Story Kirkbride) with tall towers and a Gothic edifice. Originally built to house five hundred patients with room to expand for one hundred more, the facility was called "light, airy and cheerful." The building spanned 700,000 square feet and cost $1.5 million to build. The enormous building and supporting outbuildings were constructed on Hathorne Hill, which was the former property and residence of the notorious Salem witch trial judge Jonathan Hathorne. By the 1940s, however, the facility housed two thousand patients. The small staff was unable to find additional support to help manage the asylum and resorted to ghastly methods in an attempt to keep the population under control. Shock treatment, hydrotherapy and psychosurgery were just some of the methods used on the patients. Many were also deprived of food or proper medication, while others roamed about their rooms naked and covered in their own filth. It was documented that many of the patients suffered from tuberculosis while others suffered from severe depression. Alcoholics, wives and daughters who didn't obey their husbands or fathers were committed to the facility; even women suffering the effects of menopause were signed in.

In their book *Danvers State: Memoirs of a Nurse in the Asylum*, Angelina Szot and Barbara Stillwell describe the conditions of dealing with dead patients as "eerie." One story in particular relates to the leg of a patient that was kept for further research after the patient was dead and was later buried in a separate box.

In 1992, the state finally closed the hospital, and all of the residents were removed and sent to other locations throughout Massachusetts. Between June 24, 1992, and January 12, 2005, the complex stood abandoned and quickly fell into ruin. The cemeteries on the grounds were nearly impossible to locate as they had become so overgrown with weeds, bushes and grasses, and the crude concrete markers that lie there are only inscribed with patient identification numbers. State Senator Frederick commented on the state of Danvers's cemetery in an article that ran in the *Eagle-Tribune*: "We showed no value for these souls. We dumped them in fields, covered them up and walked away."

An organization called the Danvers Memorial Committee was formed with the mission of restoring and honoring the memory of those who were buried in the cemeteries at the state hospital. The group painstakingly searched archives and state records to find out the names of those buried on the hospital grounds. On September 25, 2002, the cemetery grounds at Danvers State Hospital were dedicated, and the 768 names of the women and men buried there were read aloud. A plaque listing the patients' names and their years of birth and death was installed in the cemetery. Part of the inscription on the plaque reads: "Here rest former patients of Danvers State Hospital With love, we remember your names."

In December 2005, the property was sold to Avalon Bay Development to be converted into apartments. Despite public opposition to preserve the buildings, many of the original structures were demolished by January 2006. A small section of the original Kirkbride facility was saved, and a new structure was built behind it. In 2007, a fire broke out and destroyed four construction trailers and four apartment buildings. Currently, there are over four hundred apartments on-site, and the cemeteries are located on the lower hills of the grounds. Many visitors to the property believe that both the cemeteries and the grounds are haunted by restless spirits. Whether or not the complex is haunted, there are some who say that the memory of the hospital's patients and their experiences are eerie enough.

Northampton State Hospital Cemetery

The state asylums in Worcester and Boston had become so overcrowded by the middle of the nineteenth century that a new facility was needed for the growing population. The decision was made to build a new asylum in Northampton, Massachusetts, and $300,000 was allocated for its construction. In 1858, the facility opened under the Kirkbride plan and was designed to hold 250 patients. Much like Danvers State Hospital, by the 1940s and 1950s, the facility became grossly overcrowded, reaching a peak of 2,657 patients. In 1993, the state hospital closed. Many efforts were made to save the property from destruction. Even the mayor of Northampton committed himself to help save the buildings in 1995. All of the buildings were demolished in 2006, however, and the Kollmorgen Company built a production plant on the site.

Strangely, nearly all the records and documentation for the Northampton State Hospital have been lost. There are believed to be 594 people buried in the cemetery; others believe that there are more than 1,200 interred there. There are no stones or grave markers for the dead, and it's almost impossible to find the location unless you know where to look.

The asylum's former cemetery can be found off Route 66, in a hayfield just past the city's community gardens. There is a walking trail there, and on the trail is a small bench with two plaques that read, "State Hospital Burial Grounds 1858–1921, Rest in Peace." There is a dedication on the plaque on the other side of the monument: "Dedicated in memory of those individuals known and unknown interred on this hillside. Bench erected 1959 by William J. Goggins, Jr., Northampton State Hospital. Restored 2002 Northampton Historical Commission."

Locals have been claiming that the cemetery is haunted since the early 1950s. A group of individuals expressed interest in restoring the grounds and wanted to find out the patients' names and history, if possible. Sadly, progress has been slow, and it is uncertain how soon anything will be done to serve the memory of the forgotten souls on the hill.

Old North Church, Boston

One of the most popular stops on the Freedom Trail in Boston is the Old North Church (once known as Christ Church) located on Salem Street. Boston's oldest standing church, built in 1723, it is forever linked to the dramatic events that ignited the American Revolution. On April 18, 1775, the church sexton, Robert Newman, climbed the steeple and held high two lit lanterns as a signal from Paul Revere. The "One if by land, and two if by sea" phrase was coined by the American poet Henry W. Longfellow in his poem "Paul Revere's Ride." It was a reference to the secret signal orchestrated by Revere during his historic ride from Boston to Concord on the verge of the American Revolutionary War. The signal was meant to alert Patriots about the route the British troops chose to advance to Concord.

While visitors to the church are enthralled with touching a connection to America's rich history, they are unaware of what lies just under their feet. Within the deepest reaches of the basement of the Old North Church are the remains of more than 1,100 people. Long forgotten except by knowledgeable historians and a few archaeologists, the secrets may someday be revealed. The burial crypts date back to the 1730s, and there are many discoveries to be made within them.

Originally, the doors to the crypts were made out of wood, and as they rotted away, the bones that were held inside rolled out the doors. The bones were regularly pushed back into the crypts; eventually, they were sealed with concrete. Before long, the decision was made to dump many of the remains into a single pit, as well-paying members of the congregation wanted to be buried there. With the incidents of grave robbing at nearby Copp's Hill, the crypts underneath the church seemed a safe bet.

There are a variety of people buried in the crypts, from wealthy Bostonians to a "strangers" tomb. There is even a burial under the church altar for Timothy Cutler, who was the founding rector of the church. Gravestones with death's heads are set into the brick walls, while some tombs are marked with stone tablets with family names. Tomb 7 is marked for Captain Samuel Nicholson, who was the first commander of the USS *Constitution*. There is one open crypt that contains pieces of old wooden coffins, but where they belong, no one is sure. In Boston, history is not only visible above ground but below ground as well.

Conclusion

I have set out to include as many notable cemeteries as possible in this book and tell their stories, but there are so many other stories yet to be unearthed in Massachusetts. The opportunity to view the artwork of the hand-carved gravestones and understand their symbolic language is around every corner in Massachusetts. Cemetery ghosts wander the borders of the old burial grounds, and stories lie in hidden underground tombs. The research into the locations and stories of our forgotten burial grounds is time-consuming and sometimes frustrating but always worthwhile. The small amount of cemetery records that exists today gives us a small glimpse into our early burial traditions. However, the cemeteries themselves hold the most secrets under their soil.

I've always felt that every cemetery has a story to tell if only we could just stop and take the time to listen. Each person who is buried there has lived a lifetime of experiences, and we can connect with them through a simple visit. I sincerely invite you to start your own cemetery explorations because you never know what or *who* you'll discover.

The winding roads of Massachusetts are filled with stories of history and legend. A journey down them may lead you to make your own discoveries. This curvy road can be found in Orleans.

Bibliography

Arrington, Benjamin. *Municipal History of Essex County in Massachusetts*. N.p.: Lewis Historical Publishing, 1922.

Blackington, Alton H. *Yankee Yarns*. New York: Dodd, Mead & Company, 1954.

Bradford, Alden. *History of Bradford, Massachusetts, 1790 to 1820*. Boston: J.H. Eastburn, 1829.

Burbank, Alfred Stevens. *Guide to Historic Plymouth: Localities and Objects of Interest*. N.p.: A.S. Burbank Publishing, 1902.

Cahill, Robert. *Haunted Happenings: With New Photos of Old Ghosts*. Danvers, MA: Old Saltbox Publishing, 1992.

Cape Cod Magazine, 1915.

Clark, Rusty. *Stories Carved in Stone, West Springfield*. West Springfield, MA: Dog Pond Press, 2004.

Currier, John J. *Ould Newbury, Historical & Biographical Sketches*. Boston: Damrell & Upham Publishers, 1896.

Drake, Samuel Adams. *New England Legends and Folklore in Prose and Poetry*. New York: Little Brown and Company Publishers, 1910.

Earle, Alice Morse. *Customs and Fashions in Old New England*. New York: Charles Scribner's Publishing, 1893.

Eliot, Samuel Atkins. *History of Cambridge, Massachusetts, 1630–1930*. Cambridge, MA: Cambridge Tribune, 1913.

Gately, Paul. "Who Haunts the Sagamore Cemetery?" *Bourne Courier*, January 25, 2007.

Hawthorne, Hildegarde. *Old Seaport Towns of New England*. New York: Dodd Publishing, 1916.

Holland, Josiah Gilbert. *History of Western Massachusetts: The Counties of Hampden, Hampshire, Franklin, and Berkshire.* Springfield, MA: S. Bowles and Company Publishing, 1855.

Linden, Blanche M.G. *Silent City on a Hill: Picturesque Landscapes of Memory and Boston's Mount Auburn Cemetery.* Amherst: University of Massachusetts Press, 2007.

Ludwig, Allen. *Graven Images: New England Stonecarving and Its Symbols, 1650–1815.* Middletown, CT: Wesleyan Press, 1966.

MacDonald, Edward. *Old Copp's Hill and Burial Ground: With Historical Sketches.* Boston: Industrial School Press Publishing, 1891.

Marble, A.P. *The New England Magazine and Bay State Monthly.* 1887.

Nelson, Liz. *Newburyport: Stories from the Waterside.* Beverly, MA: Commonwealth Editions, 2000.

Perkins, Frank Herman, and Alfred Stevens Burbank. *Handbook of Old Burial Hill, Plymouth, Massachusetts: Its History, Its Famous Dead, and Its Quaint Epitaphs.* N.p.: A.S. Burbank Publishing, 1902.

Reynard, Elizabeth. *The Narrow Land.* New York: Houghton Mifflin, 1934.

Roberts, George Simon. *Historic Towns of the Connecticut River Valley.* Springfield, MA: Samuel Bowles and Company, 1855.

Sheldon, George. *A History of Deerfield, Massachusetts: The Times When the People by Whom It Was Settled, Unsettled and Resettled.* N.p.: Press of E.A. Hall & Co. Publishing, 1895.

Skinner, Charles Montgomery. *Myths and Legends of Our Own Land.* New York: J.P. Lippincott Company, Publishers, 1896.

Snow, Edward Rowe. *Pirates, Shipwrecks and Historic Chronicles.* New York: Dodd, Mead & Company, 1981.

———. *Tales of Terror and Tragedy.* New York: Dodd, Mead & Company, 1979.

Szot, Angelina, and Barbara Stillwell. *Danvers State: Memoirs of a Nurse in the Asylum.* Bloomington, IN: Author House Publishers, 2004.

Warner, Francis Lester. *Pilgrim Trails: A Plymouth-to-Provincetown Sketchbook.* N.p.: Atlantic Monthly Press, 1921.

Wheeler, Edward Jewitt, and Frank Crane. *Current Literature* 4 (January–June 1890).

About the Author

Roxie Zwicker is known for her unique collection of New England folklore and stories. She was born in Boston, Massachusetts, and grew up in New England, surrounded by its beauty and history. After attending Greenfield Community College for media production, Roxie found herself exploring the hidden secrets and forgotten history of New England. Since 1993, she has captured audiences with her fascinating storytelling abilities. In 2002, she started her own business called New England Curiosities, giving tours in New Hampshire and Maine that feature many stories from her repertoire. Roxie and New England Curiosities have been featured on the History Channel and the Travel Channel. She has hosted talks on New England legends and lore from New York to Maine and has been featured in hundreds of publications nationwide, including *Better Homes and Gardens*.

Roxie has published seven books, many of which are in their second or third printing. She hopes to keep the stories of those who settled in New England alive. For more on Roxie, visit www.RoxieZ.com and www.newenglandcuriosities.com.

Visit us at
www.historypress.net